RAC

Driver's Guide to the Law

RAC

Driver's Guide to the Law

R.H. Lawrence
Solicitor
Clerk to the Justices, Stockport Magistrates' Court

published by
Macdonald and Evans
in association with
the Royal Automobile Club

Macdonald & Evans Ltd
Estover, Plymouth PL6 7PZ

First published 1980
Reprinted 1981

ISBN: 0 7121 1285 5

Printed in Great Britain by
Butler and Tanner Ltd
Frome

Preface

Many books have been written on road traffic law. Unfortunately (in the author's opinion), the vast majority are standard text books which are somewhat difficult to read. This is not helpful to the practising lawyer, to the ordinary motorist, or to the student of law.

This book is aimed at all those who come into conflict with the law. The ordinary motorist (if there is such a person) should find in its contents the answers to questions he or she is constantly asking, e.g. "Do I have to appear in court?" "Do I need the services of a lawyer?" "Will my licence be endorsed" "Do I have to be disqualified?"

Lawyers will find within its pages the technical data so necessary for those who practise in the courts. Students of law will find the answers to many of the pre-qualification worries, such as "What is expected of me in court?"

With all of those objects in mind the book has been divided into two parts. Part I is written in a fictional style but readers should bear in mind that it is based on fact and experience. It attempts to describe an interview between a prosecuted motorist and his solicitor (sometimes itself a worry to the uninitiated). Then follows a court room scene which should help to dispel the fears of a motorist who has never been inside a court room. This topic should similarly appeal strongly to students of law and practising lawyers. Appeals are dealt with (albeit briefly) within the general contents of the book.

Part II adopts a more technical approach in a number of its chapters in that a standard text book method has been used. Nevertheless, the motorist and the lawyer will find a large proportion of Part II is written with them both in mind. Technical questions are answered and explanations given. A reference to the list of contents will indicate that many important areas of contact with the law are covered – ranging from legal aid, maximum penalties, endorsements and disqualifications to the drinking driver and the breath-alyser.

Road traffic offences are now one of the most common causes of an otherwise law-abiding person coming into conflict with the law.

It is difficult not to be able to envisage the possibility of any motorist finding himself or herself prosecuted for a road traffic offence without even trying. This is, therefore, a most important area of the law. Most such offences can only be tried by *magistrates' courts* (*see* Appendix I) and the court room scene is – as a result – at that level. Nevertheless, a reference is made, where appropriate, to Crown Court proceedings. There is justification in adopting this line if one bears in mind that over 98 per cent of all offences are dealt with by magistrates' courts and not by the Crown Court. At the same time, it must be remembered that very serious offences, such as "causing death by reckless driving", can only be dealt with by the Crown Court. Such offences amount to only a minute number of road traffic offences and they can best be dealt with in detail in specialist text books.

In summary, this book is aimed at all sections of the public. I hope that it will find a place on lawyers' bookshelves. It will, however, be in the author's view a total success if it is read by lawyers and laymen alike, not forgetting the all-important people of the future – the students.

At the end of the day a motorist stopped for a road traffic offence and told he will be prosecuted wants to know "Will I be fined?", (or worse) "Will I have my licence endorsed?"; "Will I be disqualified?" and "Can I avoid endorsement or disqualification? He may well pose these questions to his legal adviser.

The answer to some of them might lie in the discretion of the court but it might also be found within the chapters of this book.

Contents

List of Abbreviations

All E.R.	All England Law Reports
Crim.L.R.	Criminal Law Review
Cr.App.R.	Criminal Appeal Reports
J.P.	Justice of the Peace Reports
Q.B.	Queen's Bench Law Reports
R.T.R.	Road Traffic Reports

Part I

A MOTORIST IS PROSECUTED

CHAPTER 1

Advice is taken

THE INTERVIEW

Laurie Driver had wandered down one side of the street looking for the firm of solicitors, and was now strolling up the other side thinking to himself, "I know they told me at the firm that it wouldn't cost me much, and that I need a solicitor, but I've heard from other people that it can turn out to be very expensive."

Suddenly he was there! In front of him was the name plate, "Weaver, Hart and Care". He paused to wonder once more whether he was making the right decision, took a breath and then went in. His first impression was more or less as he had expected. It was a standard waiting room with one or two matchstick men on the wall which told him that the firm operated the Legal Aid Scheme. In front of him was a glass screen with a bell push. He pressed the bell and a hatch slid open. When he gave his name to the young receptionist, it was clear that he was expected. He was ushered straight into the room where Mr. Care was waiting.

"Good morning Mr. Driver. Let me take your coat and please do have a seat." The thought that ran through Mr. Driver's mind at that moment was that this Mr. Care, who had been highly recommended, appeared to be so terribly young. Could he really have the experience?

Mr. Care returned to his seat at the other side of his desk and began the expected interview.

"Now then, Mr. Driver, all I know at this stage is that you wish to see me about some summonses that have been served upon you by the police. No doubt they will tell me something about your particulars and I think it will be helpful to start there. If you can just let me have the summonses, we'll go through some of the details together. If I'm able to help you I'll need to know some facts which might seem to you to be irrelevant, so I hope you will be patient with me."

Laurie Driver reached into his inside pocket, pulled out the five well-thumbed summonses and handed them to his newly found ally. There was silence in the room for some moments while Mr. Care quickly read through the summonses. Then he looked up.

"I see the first summons is for driving without due care and attention and I presume the next three flow out of the same incident. According to the police, you failed to stop after an accident, apparently one of your tyres was defective, and you have no insurance cover. The fifth and final summons is a little out of pattern; I see it is for speeding. As it is on the same day and on the same road no doubt all the summonses arise out of the one journey. Don't bother to tell me about it just yet. Let me take down the particulars in some sort of order. Let me see: your full name is Laurie Driver and you live at 1, High Tree Avenue. I take it that you drive heavy goods vehicles as an occupation, and according to the summonses your date of birth is 27th October 1941."

Driver nodded as an answer to each question.

"Just to complete the formalities," Mr. Care continued, "Can I ask whether you are married or single?"

"I'm single," replied Driver, "but I'm hoping to be married shortly."

"How long have you been driving?" asked the young solicitor.

"Well, I have been driving for about nine years, but I've only been on heavies for about four."

"Have you got your driving licence with you?" asked Mr. Care.

Laurie Driver handed his licence over and watched his solicitor carefully. A line spread across the young solicitor's brow as he studied the two previous endorsements, which were only too plain to see. One had been recorded two years previously, when he had stopped next to a pedestrian crossing just to pop into a shop to buy a newspaper. The other was for speeding, but anyone knows how easy it is to pick up an endorsement for speeding – modern vehicles being as powerful as they are.

His solicitor looked at him and said, "Well, this is more or less as I expected. It makes life a little more difficult if one is convicted again; but, of course, we haven't reached that stage yet and perhaps never shall. You see, the point is, Mr. Driver, if we decide to go to court and fight these summonses, the magistrates are not allowed to know anything about your past record until they have found you guilty of these further allegations. Until I have some other facts, I can't predict whether they ever will reach that stage or not."

"Well, at least that's good news," thought Driver, "I've only come to see him because I am hoping that he can get me off the hook. I don't think I am guilty anyway."

Mr. Care's pen rose in the air, hovered and then came to rest over his papers. "Right," he said. " Let's move on and take down some more particulars." Mr. Care allowed Laurie Driver to tell his story in his own words, with the minimum of prompting. He explained:

"I was driving my lorry along a stretch of dual carriageway down the A1 towards Wetherby. There was a light mist and it was a bit tricky in patches. There were the usual problems with what I call weekend motorists, who either don't know what they are doing or don't seem to care; I suppose, because of that, I was taking extra care myself. All I can really say is that I'd almost reached the turning off to Wetherby when a police car came past me, put his stop sign on and pulled me into a lay-by. The copper said that I had scraped along the side of a car about four miles further back along the road. He also told me that he had checked my speed for what he said was three tenths of a mile, and that I had been travelling at about ten miles an hour over my limit.

"I don't mind telling you that I was shattered. As far as I was concerned, I hadn't been driving particularly fast, although I suppose to be fair I might have pinched an odd mile, or two, to get out of the way of the weekenders;

but as far as scraping down anybody's side is concerned, that has got to be rubbish and I told the bobby this at the time. You know what they're like, he started crawling round my vehicle but the only thing he could find wrong was that one of my inner tyres was a bit threadbare. As far as I knew it was all right when I left the depot; in any case the tyres are nothing to do with me. The firm I work for is a big enough firm to have its own maintenance depot, and they do all the checking with things like that. The bobby asked me for my insurance and I told him that insurance had nothing to do with me either and he had better get in touch with my boss. The only other thing I can remember is that he then went through the usual rigmarole of telling me that he was going to report me for possible dangerous, careless or reckless driving. He also mentioned failing to stop after an accident. Oh yes; he said something about my tyres and the insurance as well.

"I've got to be fair, he was straight enough with me and he gave me this piece of paper about producing my insurance to my local police station. Oh I forgot – he told me I was being reported for speeding. As far as I can remember, that was that. I never saw the car that I was supposed to have bumped into. I just got back into my lorry and when I eventually got back I told the depot foreman what had happened. He told me to report the matter to the boss and to mention it to the Union. The Union put me on to you and that is why I am here. I think it's all a bit stupid but I am worried to death about my licence and I just hope you can do something about it."

Mr. Care had been making notes busily during the whole of the interview. He paused from his writing and sat there for a few moments. "I don't suppose there were any witnesses that you can remember?"

"No."

"Try to cast your mind back and see whether there is anyone in your own line who might be able to help."

"No, there isn't anybody as far as I know, but I will think about it."

Again there was a pause. Then Mr. Care said:

"Well I will probably need to see you again because there

are some points that I will need clearing up, such as your own estimation as to the speed at which you were travelling; also, for example, the time you set out to pick up your load and the time you were required to get it to its destination. All that sort of thing will be helpful to show that there was no need for you to be speeding. I would like to give just a little bit more time to your problem than this, but unfortunately I am due in court shortly. There is, however, just one question that I would like to ask you and I hope you can give me an immediate reply: if not, don't worry, think about it and I will make another appointment with you before the court hearing. What I would like to know is whether you can recall any unusual noise when you were driving along the road, prior to the Wetherby roundabout?"

Laurie Driver didn't hesitate. "There was nothing at all that I can remember which could be tied up with what the policeman questioned me about. I can tell you something else too; I had the lorry checked when I got back to the depot – it's standard practice – and there were no marks of any sort on the lorry. Now that I have remembered that, I can also tell you that I asked the policeman to see if there were any marks, and he couldn't find any either."

Mr. Care looked at him thoughtfully.

"I think, before we part, I had better let you know immediately what line I propose to adopt and the advice that I would like you to follow. Let's deal with the summonses in some sort of order. The 'careless driving' and 'failing to stop' are really in effect one incident. I will have to write to the police and ask them for a copy of any statement which you have made, of which they may have kept a record.

"Unfortunately one of the problems that one is faced with in this sort of situation is that you will have to wait until you get to court to find out the strength of the prosecutor's case. The summonses issued against you can only be heard by a magistrates' court and as the law stands, at present, there is no way in which I can obtain copies of the statements of the witnesses that the police intend to call unless they choose to serve them upon you, or upon myself. Normally this is only done where their witness would be giving evidence with which you would, in any case, agree.

When this occurs the witness is not required to attend the court and the proceedings are simplified. If you don't agree with what is in a written statement served on you, then you have the right to have the witness in court, in which case the police would have wasted their time in serving the statement upon you.

"I'm only telling you this now because we're facing some difficulty concerning the 'careless driving' allegation. We won't really know what we have to face until we get to court. You don't need to worry because in practice this is quite a common situation and I will be able to deal with the matter on the day itself. I can, for example, usually discuss the substance of the allegations with the prosecutor and in any case he often outlines to the magistrates the facts which he intends to prove.

"In the case of the second summons – failing to stop after an accident – we seem to be on very strong ground and I should be able to have that case dismissed. There is, in fact, a well known reported case, at least well known to lawyers, which has bearing on this point. The name of the case is Harding against Price. The sort of situation in which you find yourself is similar to the facts of that very important appeal. I think that it will be sufficient to tell you that what was decided in that case was that you can't be guilty of failing to stop after an accident, or for that matter failing to report it, if you don't know that the accident happened. It makes common sense, doesn't it – how can you report something that you don't know about? I am confident that we will be able to persuade the court that you are not guilty of that summons. I am also reasonably happy about the summons for the defective tyre.

"The bad news, as the saying goes, is that I don't see any way of your being found not guilty of the offence because it is an offence that we lawyers call one of strict liability. In effect what the prosecution have to prove is that you were using the motor vehicle on the road and that the tyre was in some way defective. Provided they have summonsed you under the correct regulation – and they have – I am sorry to say that there is no way to avoid a conviction. The good news is that the law now allows me to put forward, on your behalf, what I call a statutory defence to any endorsement that would otherwise have to follow.

"I expect you know that the offence of using a motor vehicle with a defective tyre is an offence for which there is a compulsory endorsement. Normally the court cannot avoid endorsing your licence, unless there are reasons special to the offence itself. These reasons have to be very special indeed, but as I have said there is hope here that we can still avoid the endorsement because there is what I personally term a special defence or excuse available to you. This 'defence' can be usefully summarised as being that if you didn't suspect, or had no reasonable cause to suspect, that the defect existed, the court doesn't need to go on to endorse your licence. I think that's it in a nutshell.

"You say that you looked at your vehicle before you left the depot and didn't notice any defect and that, in any case, you have a maintenance depot with total responsibility for looking after the vehicles. I think in those circumstances we should have little difficulty in persuading the court not to endorse your licence – particularly as it was one of the inner tyres which was defective. They might conceivably still endorse and they might certainly impose a fine, but I am hopeful that even if they do fine you the amount will be nominal. I suspect that in the circumstances which you have outlined, however, they will not. So that leaves us with the fourth summons of having no third party insurance and the fifth summons of a speeding offence, which does not seem connected with the alleged accident, and which we may ask the court to deal with separately.

"I will have to make enquires as to the state of your employer's insurance policies, etc., but again, I don't think you need to worry too much at this stage. I am very confident that even if it turns out that there is something wrong with their insurance policy – and I suspect that there must be, otherwise you would not have had a summons – you can still get away with this one completely. This is because there is a statutory defence that if you reasonably believe as an employee that your employer is covered for third party insurance, then you cannot be convicted of the offence of using a motor vehicle without insurance, provided you were using it on your employer's business and upon his instructions which, of course, you were.

"The only one I am really worried about is careless driving and I hope to get more information about that and about the speeding summons. The main thing is not to worry too much at this stage until we know some more facts about the careless driving. I cannot promise you any more than that. I will try my best; but, with luck, you stand a reasonable chance of getting away with the 'failing to stop after an accident' and the insurance summonses and avoiding the endorsement on the tyre offence.

"Well, that's fine. I did mention that I would like to see you again before the court hearing and you will take it from that that I am quite happy to look after you on the 15th at the court itself. When you telephoned the office, you mentioned that you wanted to apply for legal aid. Have you filled in any forms yet?"

"No, I thought that you would have them."

"As it happens, I have, although you could have got them from the court office if you had wished. If you will just wait a few seconds in the waiting room, one of the girls will bring the forms to you to complete. One of them is a formal type of application for legal aid and on that you have to justify asking for legal aid. The court will work out whether or not you can afford to pay a solicitor yourself, whether you should pay so much towards my costs, or whether you can have my services completely free of charge. All that is really a matter of finance. From the form which you complete will be worked out how much money you have coming in and going out, and you will be given all the necessary allowances. What I want you to do is to make sure that you put on the application form some special reasons for applying for legal aid. My advice is that you ought to mention the possibility of your being disqualified and that your job depends upon your driving licence. As I have said, the court can work out for itself whether you can afford to pay something towards the legal aid costs or all the costs. It's really up to you to tell them on the form why you should be legally represented. For what it's worth, I personally don't see any reason why you should not be successful in being granted free legal aid.

I am basing that upon what you have told me about your own earnings."

They shook hands and Laurie Driver started to leave his solicitor's office. He reached the door before suddenly turning round to say:

"I think I ought to mention that, although I've got two endorsements on my licence, I've never been in court before and to be perfectly honest I'm a bit frightened about going. I've heard from my mates what happens when you get there, but you never know what to believe. If I was to take their word for it, I'd be better off pleading guilty and calling it a day. One of them said to me only yesterday that I was wasting my time. He told me about what happened when he was at court."

Mr. Care smiled. He had heard it all before and was only too well aware of his client's fears.

"I have got a few more minutes to spare before going to court, Mr. Driver. Sit down again and I will tell you very briefly what you can expect when you get to court. I will be there to help you and you will find when you are in court that there is a standard procedure for everybody to follow and you will be given plenty of opportunity to have your say. The set-up at court is something like this.

"The person bringing the proceedings against you, in this case the police, would in some courts be represented by a senior officer or by a solicitor. Sometimes the prosecutor will outline the facts which he intends to place before the court and which go towards making up the offence, but it depends upon the prosecutor and quite often upon whether or not the facts are complicated. In a large number of cases the prosecution begin straightaway by calling their witnesses. After each prosecution witness is called, I will be able to ask him questions by way of cross-examination. When the prosecutor has called all his witnesses, I can then make up my mind whether or not to submit to the magistrates that there is no case to answer at all. I might well do this where the prosecution have not proved some essential element in the offence.

"Even if I am unsuccessful at this stage it doesn't prevent me from calling you to give evidence, which really means that you can tell the whole of your side of the story to the magistrates. One of the advantages about the court system is that usually you can tell your story without interruption, but once you have had your say, then there is no doubt that you will be questioned in exactly the same way as I would question the prosecution witnesses.

"If it turns out that there are some witnesses whom I can call on your behalf then I will call them after you have given evidence. When your side of the case is finished, I will have the right to speak to the magistrates by way of a summing up of all the evidence. I will try to persuade them, if it reaches that stage, that most if not all of the summonses should be dismissed and I think we have got a very good chance with two of them.

"Assuming the worst, even if you are found guilty on the summonses, I will still have yet another opportunity to speak to the magistrates on your behalf, but then my object would be to persuade them to impose a light penalty or even perhaps no penalty at all. Unfortunately in the case of most motoring offences magistrates are expected to impose something in the nature of an arbitrary fine, because usually a person's intention is not a part of their consideration. I think I can best explain that by saying that a tremendous number of people commit motoring offences without trying and a penalty is imposed because they have committed the offence irrespective of whether they intended to commit it or not. Nevertheless, there is still a great deal of scope for me to persuade magistrates to lighten the load, particularly when they have heard all the facts in a case such as that in which you are involved.

"I think that is about all, except perhaps to mention to you that there will be at least two magistrates dealing with your case and usually there are three. The magistrates themselves in this town are not, generally speaking, lawyers. Some of them are, but they are not appointed because they are lawyers. They will have a court official with them in court sitting as their clerk and he is there to offer them advice, if necessary, on law, etc. There is really nothing at all for you to worry about. The magistrates are ordinary people and they will listen to everything which you have to say.

"Just out of interest, I can tell you that there are a large number of professional magistrates in the city areas who are either barristers or solicitors and they usually sit alone. In London, for example, you will find professional magistrates sitting regularly – they are called stipendiaries – but that is not the set-up in the court that you will be attending."

FURTHER INSTRUCTIONS

On his second visit to the solicitor's office Laurie Driver felt that he at least understood the way things were going. His solicitor might be young but he certainly seemed to know how to put him at his ease. After the usual pleasantries were over Mr. Care opened up a file on his desk. "No doubt you have heard that the court have decided to allow you legal aid, but apparently they have ordered that you make a down payment of £15 before they will issue a legal aid order."

Laurie Driver nodded. "I've been in and paid the £15 and I've got the receipt."

"Good, well now we are in business. I think perhaps I should mention to you that the £15 might not be the only money that the court orders you to pay towards your legal aid but quite often it is a guideline as to what they think you should contribute. On the other hand, if I can manage to get the cases dismissed then more often than not you will get the £15 back, but we will cross that bridge if we ever reach it."

Mr. Care paused, stroked his chin and then spoke.

"I think I'll start with the bad news first. The prosecution refused point blank to tell me anything more about the incident than what you yourself have told me. They were only prepared to say that as far as they are concerned there was an accident reported by a motorist, whose car was damaged. They more or less confirmed the conversation that you had with the policeman but I'm afraid I am not much further forward, except that I suspect that if they had evidence that your vehicle was damaged, they would probably have mentioned it to me. I don't mean that they were obstructive; it is just that I suspect that they don't know any more than I do.

"I have called that the bad news but, in fact, it is quite helpful for me to know that we are starting about equal. Most of the road traffic cases I find myself involved with at court are heavily weighted, witnesswise, against the defendant but thank goodness that magistrates don't count heads when they arrive at their decision. As I mentioned to you the last time we met, at least the procedure will allow you to have your own say.

"On the good news side, I can tell you that I've been in touch with your employers and they have arranged for me to interview the depot foreman who is responsible for the maintenance of the vehicles. In fact, I have had a chat with him over the telephone and there is no doubt that his evidence will go a long way towards your avoiding an endorsement. He accepts total responsibility as depot foreman for the state of your vehicle's tyres and is prepared to come to court to give evidence to the effect that one of his maintenance men failed to carry out a routine inspection. I feel fairly confident that we are well on the way to solving the tyre problem. I am also pleased that the foreman had the good sense to examine the vehicle personally when you returned to the garage and he could find no evidence of marks which would indicate a collision. Perhaps even better is the comment that he made to me that the load you were carrying was loosely packed and there would be a substantial amount of noise if driven at an average speed. He seems to have been involved in this sort of problem before and I think that he is going to be a most useful witness.

"Finally, I can tell you that the company secretary has confirmed that for some technical reason the insurance was not in order, but that evidence will be given by a responsible member of the firm to the effect that you would have no reason to suspect that there was no insurance cover. No doubt you will remember from when we last met that there is a complete defence to a 'no insurance' summons, where an employee can satisfy the court that he had no reasonable cause to suspect that the employer did not have the necessary cover.

"I think we are rapidly boiling it down to the careless driving and the speeding summonses. Until we get to court and I know more about the offence, I cannot offer any constructive advice at this stage, except to say that I would like you to enter a plea of 'Not guilty' to all five summonses. Usually, in these types of cases, the police decide to proceed under what is called section 1, Magistrates' Courts Act 1957. This is the procedure of which, no doubt, you have heard.

"It allows persons summonsed for comparatively minor offences to plead guilty by post. The only test is whether or not the person summonsed can be imprisoned for more than three months, and, of course, that is not the position with any of your summonses. Apart from disqualification the worst thing that can happen to you is a fine, and I would have expected the police to have used the section 1 procedure.

"The point I am trying to make is that, in section 1 cases, the police are also required to serve with the summonses a statement of the facts that they intend to allege in court; if you decide to plead 'Guilty' by post they would not be allowed to deviate from those facts. The prosecutor would be restricted by the court itself to reading word for word what was in the written statement served upon you, unless you decided to attend court and either plead 'Guilty' or 'Not guilty'. They have not used this procedure in your case, but unfortunately, it is their choice. That is why I said earlier that I suspect they don't know any more about the incident than what you have told me yourself. If they had other evidence which could be reduced into writing then I am certain that this particular police force would have served written statements on you.

"I don't suppose you will ever be summonsed again but just out of interest I'll mention to you that in minor cases of this sort you can usually write in pleading 'Guilty' even if the police have not used the section 1 procedure, but it is wise to write in sufficient time in advance to allow the court to write back and tell you that you should, if necessary, be present.

The unfortunate aspect of that is that, if it is not section 1 procedure, then your letter pleading 'Guilty' would not assist the court because the prosecution would still have to call all their witnesses. When you think about it, this is probably common sense anyway because the court could not convict you without knowing something of the facts, and that must either be provided by witnesses giving evidence, or by the written statement procedure which I have been explaining to you. I have drifted rather from the major point which I want to make to you, and that is that I would like you to go to court and enter a plea of 'Not guilty'. I'll take it from there."

Laurie Driver had sat through this part of the interview in stony silence. Some of it was a little bit too much for him to take in but at least his solicitor was now getting to the point that he had wanted him to reach from the beginning of the interview. That was whether he should plead "Guilty" or "Not guilty".

"I wanted to plead 'Not guilty' all along. I don't scc how I am guilty of any of the five summonses, although I accept what you say that I suppose we have got to wait to hear what the prosecution witnesses say in court. I feel quite a bit happier now that I know for sure that the firm are backing me up and I'm very grateful to you for all the help you have given me. The summonses said that I should be at court at ten on Tuesday morning, but I'll be doing a pick-up at the docks on that morning. Do I have to be there at ten?"

"I think you would be well advised to try to make it for ten o'clock. It will be a bit late to try to arrange an adjournment at this stage, but if it proves absolutely necessary I will do what I can."

"No, that's all right, I think I can organise things so that I can be there at ten."

"Well, that is all that I want to mention now, Mr. Driver. To coin a phrase – I will see you in court. I'll be there at about twenty to ten. I'd like to have a few words with you before you go into court, because although I have told you something about the set-up in court I would like to tell you in just a little bit more detail what is expected of you. Being in court is, on occasions, like being in a different world, in that there is the set procedure and people use strange expressions, such as 'informant' and 'defendant', but I'll tell you what I think you need to know in order for you to feel as happy as you can in strange surroundings."

They shook hands and Laurie Driver left the office feeling happier than he had felt for some days, but his day in court had not yet really begun.

CHAPTER 2

The court appearance

It had not occurred to him that when it came to being at court he might be nervous, but Laurie Driver was. "This is stupid," he thought. "Here I am, a six-foot lorry driver, used to handling heavies and I'm nervous about telling people that I've done nothing wrong, but I am." The corridor of the court was crowded and there seemed to be all sorts of types there. One man who pushed past him had tattoos on his arm, with "love" on the fingers of his left hand and "hate" on his right hand. To his relief, Laurie Driver spotted Mr. Care, who was thumbing through some papers on a notice board at the entrance to the court. Mr. Care looked round, saw his client and made his way through the crowds to greet him. They shook hands in the best traditional manner.

"Well," he said, "Here we are. Nothing to worry about. I've already told you that I'll look after you but if you would like to come and sit on this form over here I'll tell you something about what you can expect when you go in. The layout of courts may vary in different parts of the country, although the function remains unchanged. In some courts people who are summonsed actually stand in a dock arrangement but you won't have to do anything like that here; there is a small brass rail on the left hand side of the court. The court usher will call out your name, take you in and you'll have to stand temporarily just behind the brass rail. You'll see me there, but don't worry about me when you go in, just get used to the feel of the court itself and have a quick glance round you. You'll see, sitting at the front, either two or three magistrates.

"Out of interest, I would like to explain that a normal bench of lay justices consists of a minimum of two and a maximum of seven justices, unlike the stipendiary magistrates who are professionally qualified and normally sit alone. Usually, there are either two or three justices sitting in this court. Sitting in front of the magistrates is a court official – he is the court clerk. I see that the summons in your case is signed by the justices' clerk but in this particular court it won't be the justices' clerk himself who will be sitting, it will be one of his professional staff. He will probably be the first person to speak to you. He'll ask you for your name and he'll probably also ask for your address and date of birth. You can, if you wish, refuse to give him your date of birth at this stage, but you will have to divulge it if you are convicted. Wait until he asks and then tell him. Up to that point, it's simple, isn't it? What follows is also very easy.

"The clerk to the court will read the particulars of the summons to you and he'll ask you whether you plead guilty or not guilty. He'll read each summons in turn and after he reads each one, he'll ask you to plead to the summons. He'll say to you, 'Do you plead Guilty, or Not guilty?'

"To each one of them I just want you to say, 'Not guilty'. If you get nervous you can look across at me and I'll whisper the reply, or I might even answer for you. That's all that there is to the early stage of the proceedings. He'll ask you whether you are called Laurie Driver and all you'll have to say is, 'Yes, sir'. He'll then ask you whether you live at such and such an address and again all you need to say is, 'Yes, sir'. After that he'll ask you for your date of birth and you'll give it. He'll read the charges to you, one by one, and after each one he'll say, 'Do you plead Guilty, or Not guilty?' All you have to say is, 'Not guilty'.

"Nothing could be simpler because once you've pleaded 'Not guilty' to each of the summonses, all you need to do is wait until he tells you to sit down and there'll be a seat there for you. You can then leave the rest to me in the early stages. The proceedings will go something like this. The prosecuting solicitor, in this particular case, will outline the facts that he intends to prove to the magistrates. Technically, he doesn't really need to, but he will, because of the comparatively unusual circumstances in this case. Then he'll call his first witness and all you must do is sit and listen to everything that the first witness says. Right?

"I don't want you to interrupt me at all whilst the case is proceeding at that stage, but if I forget to ask what you think is a very important question, or if, for example, there is something that a witness says with which you strongly disagree and I haven't questioned him on it, then make a note of it and pass it to me. Apart from that just simply take it easy, keep calm and listen to what is being said.

"When the first prosecution witness has given his evidence it's then up to me, on your behalf, to stand up and ask him questions on what he's said. I will try to make it clear that, whilst I'm not intending to say that the prosecution witnesses are lying, their account of the incident is not sufficient for the court to find you guilty of any of the offences for which you've been summonsed. I'll do all the questioning; you just sit and listen very carefully to what is being said.

"When I've finished asking my questions, the prosecuting solicitor is allowed to ask questions to try to undo any of the harm that I might have done to his case. All the prosecution witnesses will be called one at a time and the same procedure will occur with each of them. I hope that I've made everything clear up to now. Incidentally, if I wasn't representing you and you were conducting your own case, then the same procedure would be followed, up to this point. When it came to the right to question the prosecution witnesses, you would be entitled to do it yourself. Of course, you have asked me to do it for you because I'm a professional and, I hope, I ask all the right questions.

"When the prosecution has called all its witnesses I'll be given the right to address the magistrates and try to persuade them that there is no case to answer on any, or all, of the summonses. I might be successful on at least two of them; but if not, don't worry, because then I will start to call evidence for the defence. That really means that, first of all, you will go into the witness box and you'll be asked to take the oath. You'll be told to hold the Bible in your right hand and you must read out aloud the words on the card which sets out the oath. If you don't believe in God, or if, for example, you are not a Christian but you have some other religion, then tell the clerk of the court. He'll see either that you are sworn according to your religion or, if necessary, you can affirm. An affirmation is more or less the same as being sworn; it's a promise to tell the truth.

"This is your first real speaking part. Up to now what's happened is that you've given your name and your address, you have pleaded 'Not guilty' and you've sat there listening quietly. The next stage is to go into the witness box and take the oath. This is really where you are better off by being represented by someone such as myself, because I will stand up and lead you through your evidence. In other words, I'll try to make sure that you don't forget to tell the magistrates anything which they should know about the incident itself. I've got all the notes from your interview in my office. I can't put words into your mouth. It's up to you to give your own evidence but I'll lead you through it.

"You'll find it a great help and, I hope, a comfort to have somebody there who really is on your side to make sure that everything goes properly. When you have given all the evidence that you need to give about the incident, I'll sit down. The prosecuting solicitor will then stand up and question you in exactly the same way as I questioned the witnesses. His job will be to try to show the magistrates that you are guilty of the offences. You don't need to worry; just answer the questions truthfully and keep your answers short.

"Then I'll call your witnesses. They are the depot foreman and the secretary representing the firm. They'll be asked to give evidence about the tyres and about the insurance, etc., and they'll be called in the same way as you have been called. They'll take the oath. I'll start by asking them all the necessary questions. After that they will be cross-examined by the prosecuting solicitor. In the same way as the prosecuting solicitor has had a right to come back and ask his witnesses more questions, I'll be entitled to come back at yours and undo any harm which they might have done to your case.

"Whilst your own witnesses are giving evidence, you'll be sitting quietly listening again. If they forget to say anything, you could, if necessary, make a note; but usually you'll find that if I haven't asked a question it is because the question shouldn't really be asked at all. There are some questions which are best left unasked, otherwise you might destroy the whole of the credibility of your case. When I've called all your witnesses, I will then stand up. Then I'll be able to speak to the magistrates, uninterrupted, and I'll be able to sum up everything that has been said.

"When I've finished speaking, the magistrates will probably leave the court for a short time in order to consider all the evidence that has been heard. If the magistrates speak to you on their return to the court, you should stand up immediately. It is always wise to call the chairman 'Sir', or if it's a woman 'Madam', but don't worry too much about that side of it; the main thing to remember is to stand up when they come into the room and to remain standing when they are speaking to you. They will then tell you whether they find you guilty or not guilty. If they find you not guilty, that's probably the end of the matter, except that I might be able to ask for costs to be given to you. If they find you guilty, then I'll still be able to speak to them just once more.

"This time I will speak in what is called mitigation, that is, I can put to them anything that will make the consequences of conviction for the offence less serious than it should have been. In particular, I am thinking about a possible endorsement or disqualification. If it gets to the stage of disqualification, I might have to call you back into the witness box to give a little more evidence about how it would affect you if you were disqualified; but, quite frankly, I'm very hopeful that it won't get to that stage. However, we'll have to see. Let's look at it for a few moments on the black side and I'll say this; if they are thinking about disqualifying you then you must leave it to me to try to persuade the magistrates that that is not the right thing to do."

Mr. Care had been speaking continuously for about ten minutes and it was getting very close to the time that the court was due to start its proceedings, so he closed his file and said:

"Right, now then, Mr. Driver, all I want to say for now is just to repeat once again – for goodness sake don't worry. The magistrates are ordinary people just like you or me. Their job is to listen to both sides, that is to the prosecution's side and to your side of the case. They will try their best to come to the right decision. When you go into court, just sit there and listen until you are called into the witness box; when you are called, take your time and take a deep breath, if you're nervous, before you start to speak. Once you've said the first few words you'll find everything else will flow along quite smoothly. I think you'll find that between us we will cope very well indeed.

"I'll just mention a couple of other small things before you go in. If you hear the word 'informant' used, or 'information', all that really means is this. The 'information' is the document which the police or the prosecutor have to prepare before a summons can be issued. It's just the document from which a summons is eventually issued. The 'informant' himself is not often these days the policeman who actually stopped you in the street; it will more than likely be a senior officer from the police station, who has studied the file.

"You will also hear the word 'defendant' used and that means you. Once you step into court you will be called 'the defendant' on a number of occasions; it is important that you should know that you are the defendant. You are the defendant because you are defending the proceedings, but even if you were pleading guilty, the same expression is generally used. You might hear the clerk to the court called the 'learned clerk' because he is the court's legal adviser; the prosecutor is not generally called by any special title, so just address him courteously. I don't think that I can help any more at this stage. All right now, I'll see you inside the court."

Mr. Care stood up, touched Laurie Driver on the shoulder, said, "Don't worry," and walked off down the corridor in the direction of the court.

"Blimey, that was a mouthful, " thought Driver. "At least he can talk. To be fair to him I suppose I do feel a bit better. I wonder if I can go into court and watch what's happening." He stood up and followed in the same direction taken by Mr. Care. At the end of the corridor he saw a chap standing there who looked as though he might be a court usher. "Can I go into court?" asked Laurie Driver.

"If you want," said the man who was wearing a black gown. "If you're a witness in the case, then when the case is called you will have to leave, but subject to that there is no reason why you shouldn't sit in and listen. Go through those doors there to the back of the court and sit down on the seats at the back. All right?"

Laurie Driver thanked the court usher and went through the doors as instructed. Inside the court room the furniture was laid out more or less as Mr. Care had said. On the right hand side of the court there was a large area with a brass rail surrounding it. In it were sitting three people with a policeman guarding them. Driver presumed that that was the dock for people who were in custody. In front of this secure dock arrangement was a small brass rail with a chair behind it

– he could remember his solicitor telling him that that was where he would be expected to stand because he had been summonsed. The rest of the furniture in court did not look particularly interesting to him, except that there was a small

box arrangement with what appeared to be a Bible lying on it. He assumed that that was the witness box. Just then, the court usher who had told him to come and sit in court walked in and shouted at the top of his voice, "Stand up, please." A door opened at the side and two men and a woman walked in. They took the three seats that were available at the front of the court and sat down facing the body of the court room.

"Sit down, please," said the court usher and everybody sat down. He hadn't noticed the other man come in but sitting in front of the three magistrates was a man with a young girl by his side. The man was the first to speak. He said to the three magistrates, "The first case this morning, your Worships, is the case of the police against a Laurie Driver; it's number three on your list. I understand Mr. Care appears to represent the defendant."

Mr. Care stood up and said, "That is correct, your Worships." He turned round, looked at Laurie Driver who was frozen in his seat.

"It can't be me already, surely," thought Driver. "Mr. Care said that it would be about an hour and a half before I was on, although he did say that he was going to try to get it put on earlier, because he has got to be in some other court."

He suddenly heard the clerk to the court speaking to the magistrates. "At the request of the solicitor in the next case, your Worships, would you please hear the summonses issued against a Mr. Laurie Driver? I think your Worships have already got the particulars in front of you. His solicitor has asked for a separate trial in respect of the fifth summons for speeding."

The court usher rose to his feet as soon as the clerk to the court had stopped speaking. He said at the top of his voice, "Laurie Driver". Driver rose to his feet. "Please come down here," said the court usher coming towards him to lead him down behind the brass rail. "Just stand there and listen to the clerk." Everything happened then just as Mr. Care had described, except that when it came to the stage for him to plead "Not guilty" he did feel a little uncertain as to what to do. Mr. Care was as good as his word. He stood up and said to the clerk in reply to each of the four summonses, "My client wishes to enter a plea of 'Not guilty', your Worships."

Laurie Driver sat down, as he had been instructed, and listened to the witnesses giving their evidence. He had been a little taken aback when the first witness came into the box. It was the tattooed man. He had taken the oath like a veteran. Driver found it easy enough to remember what the tattooed man said. He followed, more or less, what the policeman had said to him at the time; that he had been cut up by the lorry which had been driving on his tail for a mile or two. He told the magistrates that he had to brake because the cars in front of him braked for some reason that he couldn't see. The lorry behind him, instead of braking, pulled out, went past him at a fast speed, cut in in front of him and just managed to scrape into the space that he had left between his car and the car in front. In doing so he had caught him on the offside. He said there was a bang loud enough "to waken the dead". It was Mr. Care's turn now. When he stood up he did not really seem all that anxious to ask any questions. Such questions as he did ask seemed to be based on the weather, the age of the tattooed man's vehicle and his speed. This time Driver was concentrating pretty hard and was trying to think whether there were any other questions he should ask. He thought to himself, "Well, I suppose discretion is the better part of valour, so I'd be better off keeping quiet."

The next witness was the policeman who had pulled him into the lay-by. He seemed very bored by the whole affair but he did describe what had happened accurately enough. "At least," thought Driver, "the policeman doesn't seem biased against me." Suddenly, Driver heard the prosecuting solicitor saying to the magistrates, "That's the case, your Worships." Mr. Care immediately rose to his feet.

"I would like to make a submission of 'no case to answer', your Worships, on the summonses relating to the 'driving without due care and attention' allegation and the summons for 'failing to stop after an accident'. I'll keep my submission to the allegation of careless driving very short. You'll no doubt recall, your Worships, that when I cross-examined the first prosecution witness, who was the driver of the car involved in the alleged incident, he was asked by me whether he could recognise anyone in court, who might be the driver of the motor lorry concerned. It was hardly surprising that he should point to the defendant, that is to my client, having regard to the fact that he is sitting where he is at the present moment, but he then went on to say – and I made a note of his reply – 'I think that might have been the man, but I only caught a quick glimpse of him and I certainly couldn't be sure. All I can really remember was the colour of the lorry, which I have already told the magistrates about and I can't honestly say that he was the driver.'

"When the policeman was giving evidence, I agree that he said to your Worships that my client had conceded that he had driven the motor vehicle for about ten miles. Nevertheless, in reply to a question put by the policeman at the scene the defendant said to him that he couldn't recall the incident concerning a motor car. What is more, he said that he couldn't remember any incident on that day. The fact that he has been identified as the person named in the summons as a result of a reference to his driving licence is really not terribly relevant. I submit that there has been no evidence of identification concerning the allegation of careless driving.

"It is true that my client agrees he was driving a motor lorry on the road towards Wetherby roundabout at the time of the alleged incident. I would remind your Worships that this is an extremely busy stretch of load with lorries passing up and down it day and night. Leaving to one side the description of the colour of the motor vehicle by the first prosecution witness, there is no evidence whatsoever that the motor lorry driven by the defendant was the vehicle involved in the incident with the first prosecution witness.

"My second submission concerns the allegation of failing to stop after the accident. There are a few points to mention. The first relates to identification. I shan't repeat, however, what I have previously said because it will only cover the same ground already covered in connection with the allegation of careless driving.

"In addition to the identification questions I would like to refer your Worships to the case of *Harding* v. *Price*, a case which I am sure is very familiar to your learned clerk. I don't think I need to recite the full facts of the case. It is referred to in [1948] 1 All E.R. at page 283. It will suffice if I summarise what the Divisional Court said in that matter, which is that you can't report an incident if you don't know that it took place.

"I would also refer your Worships to one part of the police officer's evidence which agrees completely with the instructions given to me by the defendant, which is that there were no visible marks of a collision on the defendant's lorry. The lorry was inspected at the scene by both the police officer and the defendant and you recall that they both agreed that there were no visible signs of any collision.

"Furthermore, I would draw your Worships' attention to the nature of the load which was carried in the defendant's motor lorry. This was again brought out by the prosecution's own evidence. The policeman said that the defendant's motor vehicle was carrying a loose load of metal. He also agreed, under cross-examination, that the stretch of road upon which my client's vehicle was being driven was under repair in about four different stretches, and for about a total length of two miles. In particular, he agreed that the road surface where the alleged collision occurred was rough and bumpy. If one adds to that fact the type of load carried on the defendant's motor vehicle it would be hardly surprising that even if there was a slight collision this could be hidden by the combined noise from the motor vehicle and the loose metal load.

"That, your Worships, is my submission. I base it upon two specific grounds: firstly that there is no proper identification of the defendant in connection with the two summonses, to which I have referred; secondly that the summons relating to 'failing to stop after an accident' must fail because of the decision in *Harding* v. *Price*.

"I would ask your Worships to resist any temptation to put my client in peril by requiring him to give evidence because there are two essential elements missing in the prosecution's case. I shall, nevertheless, be calling my client to give evidence in respect of the remaining summonses. This is so even if you find in my favour in respect of the two to which the submission relates."

Mr. Care sat down looking quite pleased with himself. On the other hand, thought Driver, the prosecutor did not look too happy.

The clerk of the court looked towards the prosecuting solicitor and said, "Do you wish to say anything, Mr. Smith, or do you wish to reply to the submission?" The prosecuting solicitor remained silent for a few moments and then, shaking his head, said, "No, I don't think so your Worships. I'll leave the matter with you."

The chairman leaned forward and had a whispered consultation with the clerk of the court. Laurie Driver looked across at his solicitor who merely shrugged his shoulders and waved one hand as if signalling him to be silent. Laurie Driver now noticed that the chairman was whispering to the magistrate on his left hand side who nodded. There was a similar consultation with the magistrate on the chairman's right who also nodded. The chairman started to write something on a piece of paper in front of him. Laurie Driver was now getting a little nervous and moved forward in his seat to speak to Mr. Care. However, he never managed to open his mouth, because the chairman was starting to speak.

"Mr. Care," he said, "it will be sufficient, I'm sure, if I say to you that we agree with your submission; therefore the two summonses alleging careless driving and failing to stop after an accident are both dismissed."

As soon as the chairman had started to speak Mr. Care had risen to his feet. He glanced quickly across at the defendant and gave him a slight smile. He then faced the magistrates, gave a small bow and said, "As your Worships please. I would now like to call the defendant to give evidence in respect of the remaining summonses." This was the moment for which Laurie Driver had been waiting. He could feel himself going hot and cold. He couldn't remember what Mr. Care had said about the next stage. Fortunately the court usher had by this time walked round to his side, tapped him on the arm and said, "Just go into the witness box."

Everything then happened rather quickly. He walked into the witness box and before he could gather his thoughts the clerk of the court said to him, "Hold the Bible up in your right hand and read out aloud the words on the card." Laurie Driver had thought of telling them that he didn't believe in God but decided it wasn't the right time or place; so he merely swallowed and read the words out aloud. He couldn't remember whether he held the Bible in his right or his left hand, but no-one commented so it did not seem to matter.

Mr. Care had been right. In fact, he had been right about everything up to now. Laurie Driver found the first part of his evidence was comparatively easy, because his solicitor led him through it. There were some facts which he had forgotten but Mr. Care prompted him.

He didn't enjoy being cross-examined at all. The prosecuting solicitor seemed anything but friendly. He was polite enough but a very persistent man. He went on and on about the fact that Laurie Driver should have inspected the vehicle's tyres before he drove out on that day's journey. He asked why the load was loose and who had loaded the vehicle. There were a thousand and one other questions, all of which rattled Laurie Driver a little.

The cross-examination came to an end and the questioning returned to good old Mr. Care. "It's funny how someone seems to be older when you have confidence in him," thought Driver. Mr. Care put everything right during what he called "re-examination" . Driver thought "re-examination" was a funny expression, but it seemed to mean that you were given a chance to explain any part of the evidence that you had made a mess of during cross-examination. Laurie Driver was pleased when he could leave the witness box and go back to his seat. He settled into his chair feeling somewhat relieved at having got his evidence over.

Mr. Care then called the foreman of the depot into the witness box. Laurie Driver's attention wandered slightly and he found himself thinking that he had not made such a bad job of telling his side of the story to the magistrates. This was probably because they really did look like ordinary people. At least they were dressed in ordinary suits – and they didn't have wigs on, which is what he had expected. He brought his mind back to the court. The foreman of the depot, who was responsible for vehicle maintenance, seemed to be doing a pretty good job.

"I'll have more time for him in future," thought Driver, "He certainly seems to be highly qualified." At this point

Mr. Care was asking the foreman of the depot to describe to the magistrates the usual procedure carried out in respect of maintenance of the motor vehicles. The foreman seemed confident enough. He quickly told the magistrates that the tyres were changed regularly. He handed to the clerk of the court some papers which proved that there was what he described as regular maintenance. "I like that," thought Laurie Driver. The foreman of the depot then produced a book which showed that the lorry had had a complete tyre change on all wheels about three weeks before Laurie Driver had been stopped. The foreman's evidence was soon over. The cross-examination of his evidence had seemed to be harmless enough.

Mr. Care then called the company secretary into the witness box. He told the magistrates that the company was normally fully insured in respect of their seven motor lorries. He said that he didn't regard it as any business of the drivers employed by the firm to question him upon matters such as insurance. He also explained to the magistrates that he would expect all his employees, including the defendant, to believe that the firm was insured. Apparently what had gone wrong was of a contractual nature between the firm, the insurance brokers and the insurance company. It had since been put right. He then produced a letter from the insurance company to say that the firm would have been covered by insurance even if there had been an accident.

Under cross-examination he said that it was not a question of being wise after the event. He went on to tell the court that the insurance company had agreed that in the event of the defendant being convicted of the offence of careless driving or at any later stage being found to have some civil liability then they would pay out under the policy.

Laurie Driver listened to the company secretary saying that he hoped that even if the court did find the defendant guilty of any of the offences for which he had been summonsed they would deal with him leniently and that so far as the firm was concerned he was a very good worker.

"That's fine," thought Driver. "I wonder what's next?" He only had a few seconds to wait before Mr. Care rose to his feet.

"That's the case for the defence, your Worships. I hope to be able to keep my address to you quite short. I am relying upon two points of law. From the outset my client, the defendant, has admitted that he was using the motor lorry at the time of the alleged incident. About that fact there is no dispute. Nevertheless, I would like to refer your Worships (and I have got no doubt at all that your learned clerk has anticipated this point) to section 143(2) of the Road Traffic Act 1972. This section clearly allows the defendant to put forward to you a statutory defence to a summons for using a motor vehicle without third party insurance. The relevant part of the section reads thus:

> 'A person charged with using a motor vehicle in contravention of this section shall not be convicted if he proves that the vehicle did not belong to him and was not in his possession under a contract of hiring or of loan, that he was using the vehicle in the course of employment and that he neither knew nor had reason to believe that there was not in force in relation to the vehicle such a policy of insurance or security as is mentioned in subsection (1).'

"In summary, I suggest that the section clearly means that if an employee is using a motor vehicle on his employer's business, under his instructions or with his authority, and at the time he is using the motor vehicle the employee reasonably believes that his employer is covered in respect of insurance for such use, then this is an absolute defence to the charge. The only issue, your Worships, is whether you are satisfied that there was reasonable belief on the part of the defendant that his firm had the necessary insurance cover. I would urge your Worships to accept the evidence of the secretary of the company, which is, I submit, adequate to deal with this point. I would, therefore, ask your Worships to dismiss the summons for no third party insurance.

"This leaves the summons for using a motor vehicle with a defective tyre. I accept (and in any case I am sure you will be advised by your learned clerk on this point) that this is, in effect, an absolute offence. It is an offence of strict liability. I think the most I can do, as far as the offence itself is concerned, is to urge your Worships as strongly as I possibly can to consider granting the defendant an absolute discharge. I put this to you, and I hope that you agree with me, that this is one of those offences where the defendant is legally liable and yet at the same time morally blameless. This is exactly the point that was decided in the case of *Hart* v. *Bex* [1957], on page 622 of the *Criminal Law Review*, which was a case concerning a defective braking system. The Divisional Court said that in such circumstances the court must, of course, record a conviction because of the absolute nature of the offence itself; but they should, nevertheless, impose a sentence which would not, except for a limited purpose, rank as a conviction. For that reason, your Worships, I do ask you to consider most carefully whether or not this is a proper case in which you should not impose any penalty upon my client and that you should grant him an absolute discharge.

"Unfortunately, even if you agree with me, this does not avoid what is then the remaining obstacle – whether or not my client's licence should be endorsed. I appreciate that you have not finally decided upon the matters in issue, but in addition to the points as to which I have already addressed you, can I, respectfully and finally, draw your attention to Schedule 4 to the Road Traffic Act 1972? The Schedule sets out the many offences contained in the Act. In particular it details the penalties which can be imposed and whether or not disqualification and/or endorsement is applicable. Perhaps your learned clerk will show you a copy of this Schedule whilst I am addressing you on this point. You will see in the fifth column that there is what I would describe as a defence to what would otherwise be compulsory endorsement in respect of the summons for a defective tyre. The defendant must satisfy you that he didn't suspect and had no reasonable cause to suspect that the defect existed.

"Can I, therefore, remind you briefly of part of the evidence which was given by the foreman of the depot at which the defendant is employed. The foreman, you will recall, is responsible for the maintenance of the vehicles generally but in particular he referred to the system of maintaining the tyres. He said in evidence that the drivers themselves have no responsibility of any sort for ensuring that the tyres are in good condition, except the sort of responsibility that is placed upon every driver. Naturally, your Worships will also have regard to the evidence given by the defendant himself on this particular point. Again I hope you will bear with me if I remind you that, under oath, he said that he did walk round the vehicle before setting off on his journey; he did test the lights and at that stage noticed no defect in the tyres, or for that matter any mechanical defect in the vehicle itself.

"The defective tyre was defective only so far as part of the tread itself is concerned and it appears to have been caused through a badly balanced wheel. Because of the number of wheels on this particular vehicle I would ask you to say that it is reasonable to expect the driver to carry out some sort of visual inspection; but that defect may perhaps not be able to be observed because it is wrongly positioned at the time of inspection – for example, the defective part of the tyre might have been against the road surface. In addition, this was one of the inner wheels which are most difficult to inspect without proper equipment. In circumstances such as I have just outlined, your Worships would be quite entitled to come to the conclusion that my client, the defendant, has carried out both his legal and moral obligations.

"I submit to you, your Worships, that this is a reasonable explanation as to why the defect was not observed by the defendant before he set out upon his journey. Having regard to all the evidence, including the evidence put forward by the prosecution itself, I would urge you that even if you do convict the defendant in respect of the offence of using the motor vehicle with a defective tyre, then I would ask you seriously to consider granting him an absolute discharge. If you are not in agreement with me as to the nature of the penalty which should be imposed, if indeed there ought to be any penalty at all, then I would further ask you to have regard to the provisions of Schedule 4 and not to order the defendant's licence to be endorsed."

Mr. Care stopped speaking, glanced quickly at the notes which he had been making, gave a slight smile in the direction of the clerk and a bow in the direction of the magistrates and then sat down.

Driver found himself wondering what was going to happen next. He had not quite followed all that had been said which dealt with the law, but he had followed the major line of argument that he should not be convicted of the offence of having no third party insurance and that even if he was guilty of the defective tyre summons there was a good chance that his licence wouldn't be endorsed. Things looked bright. There was a movement from the clerk who stood up and whispered something to the chairman. The chairman turned to his colleagues, then stood up and said, "The court will adjourn for a few moments."

"Stand up please," said the court usher. Everyone rose to their feet whilst the magistrates left the court.

"Blimey, what on earth is happening now," thought Driver. Mr. Care came over and said this.

"Well, I think, with any luck at all, we're on a winner here with all four. But you can never tell your luck and the magistrates might not agree. More likely than not, they will send for their clerk and he'll offer them some advice on the points which I've raised, but they are points with merit and we'll just have to wait and see now. Keep calm. I don't think they'll be too long."

Driver could not leave it at that. He took Mr. Care's hand and shook it.

"Well, whatever happens, thanks very much for all you've done up to now. I should tell you that I wasn't too happy when the case started, but I'm glad I came to see you. I know that you told me right from the very beginning, or somebody did, that I could do it all myself. I suppose I could have done a bit of it here and there but I don't think I would have stood a chance when it came to speaking to the magistrates as you did at the end. I suppose that's what being a professional is all about. On the other hand, I would have liked to have had a go at asking that tattooed lad some questions, because he needed a piece of my mind. If he didn't need a piece of my mind now I would have liked to have seen him there and then at the scene and then I could have told him what I thought of him."

Mr. Case smiled and said, "Yes, I know how you feel, Mr. Driver, and I'm sure I would feel exactly the same way myself, but in actual fact it was lucky that you didn't see him at the scene, because you might have said something then that wouldn't have looked well in court. As it happens, you had most things on your side so let's wait and see what the magistrates decide."

Driver turned his head because he saw the clerk leaving the court. "Where's he going?" he asked.

"Well, either he thinks that there are some points of law involved here, upon which the magistrates need advice – and, to be fair, there are, because I have raised them – or alternatively the magistrates have sent for him. With talking to you, I didn't really notice, but it's all right, in this particular case he's got a right to be in the magistrates' room and with any luck at all it'll be an advantage if he is there. He'll be able to draw the magistrates' attention to the necessary sections and then he can leave them to make up their own minds."

Mr. Care turned on his heel and walked over to the prosecuting solicitor. "That's funny," thought Driver. "A few minutes ago they seemed to be on opposite sides; now they are quite friendly; still I suppose those are the rules of the game."

The door at the side of the court opened. The court usher shouted, "Stand up please." The same three magistrates trooped back into court and everything followed the same pattern as before. The magistrates and the clerk, who had returned to the court at the same time, took their seats. The court usher shouted, "Sit down please," and everybody sat down, except Driver who remembered what Mr. Care had said and remained standing. The chairman looked across at Laurie Driver. There was a slight pause and then the magistrate spoke for the first time to Driver himself.

"Mr. Driver, we have listened very carefully indeed to everything that your solicitor has had to say; I must make it clear to you here and now that he has managed to persuade us, firstly, that the summons for using a motor vehicle without third party insurance ought to be dismissed, and secondly, that although we must find you guilty of the offence of using the motor vehicle with a defective tyre, we feel that the blame, such as it is, attaches to your employers and not to you as an employee. We therefore order that you be granted an absolute discharge in respect of the offence. That means that there will be no penalty imposed upon you at all today. In addition we accept what has been said to us by your solicitor and your licence will not be endorsed."

The chairman looked away from Laurie Driver and spoke to his solicitor. "Mr. Care."

Mr. Care rose to his feet. "Yes sir."

"I understand that when the case started earlier this morning you indicated to our clerk that you wished to elect for a separate trial in respect of exceeding the speed limit. This can now take place. The clerk has advised us that you have a right, if you wish, to a separate bench. Can you tell us, exactly, what is your intention?"

"Well, firstly, I would like to thank you and your colleagues for the care that you have taken in respect of the summonses that you have heard to date. In all the circumstances my client would be more than happy that you should continue to hear the remaining summons, but before any evidence is called, can I explain to you that the reason why I asked for a separate trial, was because I advised my client that this was, in effect, a completely separate matter from the other four issues and that it would be best if it was dealt with as a separate entity. I can also say to you, your Worships, that it will only be an extremely short matter because I accept most of the facts that are going to be put forward by the prosecution. Nevertheless, I will have to ask for evidence to be called, simply because the prosecution decided, in this case, not to adopt the plea by post procedure and, therefore, before my client can properly decide how to plead he, and of course I, would like to hear the prosecution's evidence. My learned friend can, however, keep the matter short and I would have no objection to his leading the witnesses, except on the matter of actual speed."

"Thank you, Mr. Care," said the chairman. He looked down at the clerk to the court. "Would you put the speeding summons to the defendant, Mr. Clerk." The clerk looked straight at Laurie Driver.

"It's alleged that you exceeded the speed limit on the same

date as the other incidents. Do you plead 'Guilty' or 'Not guilty'?"

Laurie Driver once again was confused. He looked across at Mr. Care. His solicitor immediately rose to his feet and said to the clerk to the court, "My client enters a formal plea of 'Not guilty', your Worships."

The clerk seemed to accept that and wrote something on the papers in front of him. He waved his hand at Laurie Driver, which appeared to be a signal to sit down, so Driver sat. He was starting to feel almost comfortable in the court and he was able to watch the proceedings with a lighter heart. The policeman came back into the witness box and took the oath. His evidence was over in moments. He gave evidence about following Laurie Driver and mumbled something about checking him over an even distance. He then gave evidence about his speedometer having been checked.

The thing that stuck in Laurie Driver's mind was that the policeman alleged that he was driving about ten miles per hour over the speed limit and overtaking vehicles in the nearside lane. Driver thought to himself, "Well, I suppose that's possible but it's a little bit unfair because I was carrying a heavy load and the spot that he was talking about was downhill. The problem is, I don't think I'm going to be able to argue about it."

He heard Mr. Care saying to the court, "No, I don't wish to ask the officer any questions, thank you." Mr. Care came over to where Driver was sitting. He said, "I haven't asked the policeman any questions because he only said what we anticipated he was going to say anyway. All I really want to ask you at this stage is whether you strongly disagree with what the policeman said. If so, do you want to go into the witness box and tell the magistrates that you were only going at the proper speed?"

This conversation was whispered, so Laurie Driver kept his voice low as well.

"No, I was thinking while the policeman was giving evidence that there isn't any way that I can say that he's wrong. I'm a little bit surprised but I can remember that this was a downhill stretch and if I was overtaking vehicles it is possible that I clocked it up a bit. I think it's a bit unfair to book me at that particular stretch, because with the other endorsements on my licence, quite honestly, I've been taking it easy; but I don't think that there is any point in me trying to argue."

Mr. Care nodded. "I agree Mr. Driver," he said. "I think we've got a good bench here and it would be a little bit unwise to upset them. My advice to you, and I hope you'll accept it, is to let me change your plea formally from one of 'Not guilty' to one of 'Guilty'." Laurie Driver felt a little bit sick at this but nodded.

Mr. Care returned to his seat. "Thank you, your Worships, for allowing me that short break to take further instructions from my client. I can now inform you that having heard what the prosecution have to say the defendant would now like to change his plea from one of 'Not guilty' to one of 'Guilty'." The clerk immediately spoke.

"Laurie Driver," he said. "Stand up, please." Laurie Driver rose to his feet. "Laurie Driver." The clerk was speaking again. "I must read the summons to you again so that you can, if you wish, reconsider your plea. You are summoned for exceeding the speed limit contrary to section. 78, Road Traffic Regulation Act 1972. Do you now plead 'Guilty' or 'Not guilty'?"

Driver again looked across at Mr. Care, who, like the professional he was, was already on his feet. "The defendant would like to enter a plea of 'Guilty', your Worships, and I enter that plea on his behalf." The clerk, who seemed to accept this as normal procedure, nodded, made a note on his papers and said to Mr. Care, "In that case, Mr. Care, do you wish to address the magistrates further?"

Mr. Care said, "Yes, thank you, sir. Your Worships have been very patient with me this morning and I trust that I can assist by keeping the matter fairly short. The defendant deserves, your Worships, considerable credit for his honesty in this matter. It must have been very clear to you, as the case proceeded, that the man you have in front of you has accepted any blame attached to him without argument and this pattern has been followed in this particular summons.

The problem that now faces him, and once again I trust this will be partly in his favour, lies in the fact which I must disclose to you immediately. He has two previous endorsements upon his licence. The first is for parking within the limits of a pedestrian crossing and the second is for speeding. Both of these were committed within the relevant three-year period."

Laurie Driver heard the clerk speaking.

"Mr. Care, I am sorry to interrupt you, but I think it is sometimes a little misleading to use the words, 'committed during the relevant three-year period'. The court is only concerned as to whether the endorsements on the defendant's driving licence were ordered to be recorded on his driving licence within the three years immediately preceding the commission of this offence. I know that you appreciate this, but I'm saying this for the benefit of your client as well. One must look at the date of the present speeding offence, and then at the date of the convictions which are endorsed on the defendant's driving licence. The dates of the actual endorsements for the two previous offences are the relevant dates, not the dates on which the previous offences were committed. If the present offence of speeding was committed during the three years following those two previous endorsements being placed on his licence, then he is liable to compulsory disqualification for a minimum period of six months under section 93, subsection (3) of the Road Traffic Act 1972." The clerk put down his pen.

"Good grief!" thought Laurie Driver, "The clerk hasn't said a great deal up to now but I can see that he is obviously a lawyer and knows his stuff." Mr. Care did not seem unduly perturbed by the course of events.

"I'm very grateful indeed, your Worships, for what your learned clerk has said and, of course, he is absolutely right. I do apologise for the rather loose wording which I used but that is, nevertheless, the situation of the defendant. If you look at the present offence for speeding, you will see that it was committed on 1st April 1978. I will hand the defendant's driving licence to your learned clerk and he will be able to show you that the endorsement for parking within the limits of a pedestrian crossing was recorded on the defendant's driving licence on 28th February 1976 and the second endorsement for speeding was recorded on the defendant's driving licence on 24th September 1977.

"Clearly, therefore, on the date when the defendant committed this latest offence of speeding, he already had two previous endorsements recorded on his licence. He is, therefore, liable to possible compulsory disqualification for a minimum period of six months. I say possible (I can see that your learned clerk is going to speak to me once again) because I am entitled to put to the court any circumstances which would mitigate the normal consequences of the penalty, that is the normal consequences which would follow this present conviction. There are, your Worships, I would submit to you, the strongest possible mitigating circumstances, some of which relate to the offence and some of which relate to the offender himself, and under this particular section I am sure your learned clerk will agree that I can put forward any circumstances which will go towards mitigation, whether they relate to the offence or to the offender."

The clerk spoke again. "Quite right, Mr. Care, but if you are putting forward mitigating circumstances, this court will expect you to call some evidence on oath to support them."

"But of course, sir," said Mr. Care, "That is precisely what I intend to do, but before calling the defendant to give evidence I would like to explain in summary what the mitigation amounts to."

"Please carry on, Mr. Care," said the chairman.

"Thank you sir" said Mr. Care. "In short, the mitigation is as follows. Firstly, as far as the speeding itself was concerned, you have heard several times this morning that the defendant was carrying a heavy load. The stretch of road where the speeding offence was committed is well known to you and I am sure, your Worships, that you will recall the particular part of the dual carriageway leading to this roundabout has a downhill stretch some miles before the roundabout itself. The vehicle immediately in front of the defendant's motor lorry was travelling at a slower speed than the limit itself. According to the instructions given to me by my client in my office, the speed of the vehicle in front of him was about ten miles per hour slower than the actual limit. There was a gap between that vehicle and the other vehicles. The gap was starting to widen so the defendant, upon seeing that he had an opportunity to overtake, pulled out and started to overtake the vehicle in front of him.

"What happened next must have happened to all of us. As soon as he started to overtake, the private motor car started to accelerate and the gap between his vehicle and the vehicles in front lessened. The defendant was unable to pull back into his nearside and although he should have braked and gone back to his original position he unwisely continued to overtake not only that vehicle but all the other vehicles in the line. He never increased his speed from the speed which was necessary to overtake the vehicle which put him in this predicament and presumably it was at this time that the police car started to check his speed and the offence occurred.

"I would, therefore, ask your Worships to take account of the fact that when the defendant originally pulled out to overtake, even if he was going to exceed the speed limit at that time through necessity, it would have only been for a brief moment and that the rather prolonged nature of the speeding was caused by a matter somewhat out of his control. He does, nevertheless, offer his apologies to the court. He has asked me to say to you that since his last two endorsements he was only too well aware of the consequences of any further speeding and has, therefore, been taking extra care despite the many thousands of miles that he travels yearly. It wasn't, therefore, your Worships, a question of the defendant merely putting his foot down and exceeding the speed limit. He agrees that he exceeded the speed limit but he does feel that there are circumstances to put forward which are worthy of some mitigation on the part of the court.

"The second area of his mitigation is one which is also very familiar to you; if he is disqualified, this is likely to put his future employment in jeopardy. We are not talking here about a large firm, at least not when one compares the firm with other haulage contractors. I am authorised by the company secretary to say that whilst they would be most reluctant to dispense with the services of Laurie Driver it might well be that that would be the only possible result of a lengthy period of disqualification.

"I can put it to you no higher than that at this stage, your Worships, because, of course, whether or not the defendant is dismissed from his employment will depend very much on your decision. I do hope that you will see fit to take such action as is consistent with your judicial duties to allow the defendant to continue driving his motor lorry. The defendant is not married and I can't therefore put forward to you the usual problems facing drivers of heavy goods vehicles – that it would also affect his wife and family – but he is engaged and is hoping to marry within the next few months, your Worships.

"I would restrict my mitigation to those two points. Firstly that there is, I would submit, a huge area for sympathy as to why the defendant is before you for exceeding the speed limit; and secondly, in these days of high unemployment it would indeed be a shame to add to it by putting off the road a man who is clearly a most competent and professional driver. In saying this I would direct your attention to the nature of the two previous endorsements, neither of which have been for any element of bad driving, and indeed today by your own decision you have shown that his licence still remains free from any stain relating to bad driving."

Mr. Care then turned his head, nodded towards Laurie Driver and said, "I'll now call the defendant into the witness box, your Worships."

Laurie Driver knew the way and went straight into the witness box. The court usher put the Bible into his right hand and Laurie Driver read the words from the card. He was much happier than the first time he went into the witness box. Mr. Care was speaking to him.

"Mr. Driver, you've heard what I've said. Is it all correct?"

"Yes sir."

"Is there anything you wish to add?"

"No sir."

"In that case, your Worships, that's all I wish to say on this matter."

The clerk of the court glanced over towards the prosecuting solicitor and said, "Do you wish to ask the defendant any questions?"

The prosecuting solicitor rose to his feet and said, "No thank you sir, I'll leave the matter to your Worships."

The clerk then looked at Driver and said, "Please return to your seat."

He walked back thinking to himself, "Well, I wonder what that was all about. I didn't seem to have to say very much, I was just confirming what Mr. Care said. On the other hand, I agree with what he said, so I suppose that's all right." There was a shuffle of chairs and he turned his head and saw that the magistrates were standing up. At the same time he heard the court usher say, "Stand up please." Once again the magistrates disappeared through the door at the back of the court. Mr. Care came back over to speak to him.

"It's in the lap of the gods, Mr. Driver – so to speak. It's not quite so high as that but it's certainly out of our hands now."

"Well, I suppose you couldn't have done any more," said Driver. "What happens now?"

Mr. Care simply said, "Well, nothing until we hear the decision. If it goes against us then I'll offer you some futher advice; if it goes in our favour then we can thank our lucky stars. I know this court well. Unfortunately the clerk advises them along lines with which I don't agree but with which I can't argue. He knows the law and what he says, in effect, is that section 93 of the Road Traffic Act, which is the section that is causing us the problem, says that if you are before the court for an offence committed within three years of two previous endorsements being placed on your licence then the court must start on the basis that you have got to be disqualified. That is compulsory. It is for a minimum period of six months for each endorsable offence before the court upon which you are convicted. In other words, the law says that the disqualification can be for longer than six months consecutive for each offence that comes within the scope of section 93.

"In your case it could now be a minimum period of six months but if you had had your licence endorsed for the defective tyre offence it could have been six and six consecutively making twelve months disqualification in total. The disqualification also runs consecutively to any other to which you might then be subject, but that doesn't apply to you. It can, however, be shorter if you can satisfy the court that there are circumstances which would mitigate the normal consequences of the conviction. In other words, the normal consequence is a minimum disqualification of six months.

"The magistrates are very fair. I think there is a chance, a very good chance, that they will accept what has been put forward on your behalf as good mitigation. The trouble is that they regularly hear that people are going to lose their jobs. They tend to regard that as an excuse rather than a reason. Some courts even take the view that the professional driver ought to be more careful than the ordinary driver who is not on the road so regularly; I suppose there is something in that argument.

"The reverse side of the coin, however, is that the professional driver is on the road so regularly that it becomes fairly easy for him to pick up endorsements. The strength of your mitigation, in my opinion, is that your previous endorsements have not been for bad driving. Whilst it is true to say that a professional driver can collect endorsements very easily, at the same time courts do look at the nature of the endorsement that he has collected. It's always a small point in your favour if it's not for bad driving."

"Well, I hope they don't disqualify me," said Driver "because I've been on the roads almost since I got my licence. I'm not really sure what I will do if I can't drive."

"Yes I appreciate that, but let us not worry about it until it happens. Let's just wait and see what the magistrates decide."

At that moment the magistrates came back into court, together with their clerk. The clerk went to his seat and, after the usual standing up and sitting down ceremony, the clerk spoke.

"Mr. Care," he said, "I think it's only right for me to let

you know that I have been advising the magistrates on the law as to mitigating circumstances. One of the points I put to them was that you did call the secretary of the company to court to give evidence in this case. On the other hand, you haven't seen fit to re-call him as to whether or not the defendant will lose his job. It's entirely a matter for you; I have been asked by the magistrates to draw to your attention the omission in case you had just simply forgotten."

Mr. Care had turned somewhat red. He hesitated slightly, which in itself was a little unusual for him.

"I do apologise most sincerely, your Worships, it was a complete oversight on my part. I think it was probably with separating the cases and having separate trials. Certainly it was my intention all along to call the secretary and if you will permit me I will bring him forward now."

The chairman of the magistrates nodded and said, "Yes please Mr. Care, we would like to hear from the secretary."

The company secretary had been sitting at the back of the court all this time and he came forward. It crossed Laurie Driver's mind that he might not be too pleased at having been kept waiting all this time. He just hoped that he was still in the same good mood that he appeared to be in earlier in the day. The company secretary took the oath and gave his name a second time. Mr. Care said to him, "I don't propose to go over everything that I have already said. Can you perhaps help the magistrates on a final but very important point. Will you be forced to dismiss the defendant if he is disqualified from driving or might it be possible to employ him in some other capacity?"

The secretary paused for some moments. The silence worried Driver.

"Well, it's really a very difficult question to answer at this stage. It rests, I suppose, on the length of the disqualification. Anything more than two months' disqualification will force us to dispense with Laurie Driver's services even though we consider him to be an extremely good employee. Anything less than two months and the company would consider keeping him with us. Unfortunately, the over-all employment situation is so uncertain, as no doubt your Worships know, that I am afraid I cannot guarantee that he would be able to stay with the firm. I do say that with some reluctance because he is very highly regarded. On the other hand, I must be realistic and say that there can be no guarantee that he will be able to remain in the employment of the company."

Mr. Care looked a little unhappy but simply said, "Thank you, sir, for coming to help the court in this way."

Again the secretary returned to his seat.

The magistrates, without saying anything further, rose from their seats and automatically everyone else in court stood up. Driver watched the magistrates walk out of the court.

Mr. Care came over and said, "I am sorry for that. I'm not sure why but I completely forgot about recalling the secretary. On reflection it's probably in our favour anyway because it shows that the magistrates are very reluctant to disqualify you. If they had been intending to disqualify you then you would be disqualified now, but they did at least give me the chance to call the further evidence. Nevertheless, it doesn't mean that you are out of the wood. I suspect that disqualification is still on the cards. Keep your fingers crossed." Mr. Care returned to his seat.

By this time Laurie Driver was getting more than anxious about the whole proceedings. He just wanted to get out of court and go home. He wondered to himself, "How long will they be?"

The magistrates were out for about thirty minutes. It was one of the longest half-hours that Laurie Driver could remember. When they came back into court he sensed that all had not gone well.

The chairman looked at him, looked away and then looked back a second time. Driver had remembered to remain standing. The chairman spoke.

"Mr. Driver, you will appreciate that we have taken considerable care with your case but we are forced by the terms of section 93 to disqualify you for a short period of one month. The law requires that we must explain in open court our reasons for mitigating the normal consequences of the conviction. We feel that there would be excessive hardship caused to you by a longer period of disqualification.

We would also like to depart from our normal practice and say that it is the wish of us all that the firm gives some thought to keeping you in their employment, albeit in some other capacity, during your period of disqualification.

"Let me tell you, Mr. Driver, that you have been extremely lucky. It was in our minds to disqualify you for the full period of six months, and you have Mr. Care to thank for the shorter period of disqualification. In addition to disqualifying you for the period of one month we are also ordering you to pay a fine of £25. Your licence will, of course, be endorsed. That, Mr. Driver, is the sentence of the court – you are to be fined £25, have your licence endorsed and be disqualified from holding or obtaining a driving licence for one month. I must also remind you that under no circumstances must you drive during your period of disqualification otherwise the consequences, for you, will indeed be most serious."

The chairman looked away from Laurie Driver and spoke to Mr. Care. "Perhaps, Mr. Care, you would like to take instructions as to how the fine is to be paid. Please also make sure that his driving licence is handed to the clerk of the court. As you know, Mr. Care, the licence will have to be forwarded to the Driving Licence Department at Swansea, who will retain it during the period of the disqualification. The defendant can obtain his driving licence back from the Swansea Centre as soon as his disqualification has ended."

"I will, your Worships."

What followed next was a little hazy to Laurie Driver. He could remember Mr. Care asking the court whether he could have one month to pay and the court saying that it ought to be paid by instalments of £5 per week otherwise Mr. Driver would be brought back before the court. Laurie Driver left the court feeling a little shaken, mainly because he was not really quite sure what was going to happen to his future employment. He waited in the corridor outside for Mr. Care. His solicitor joined him some five minutes later.

"Well I know that you are feeling a little unhappy just at the moment, Mr. Driver, but when you have got time to think about it you will realise just how very lucky you've been. When we walked into court this morning we were facing five summonses. I can tell you that if you had been convicted of them all the minimum disqualification that you would have been liable to suffer would have been two and a half years. That is what you would have been liable to because of section 93 of the Road Traffic Act. It lays down six months for every offence for which your licence is liable to be endorsed and you were facing five endorsements this morning. You have got off three of the summonses completely and for the fourth one, for a defective tyre, there was no endorsement ordered. It was only on the speeding summons that you were facing endorsement. Now that isn't bad when you come to think about it, is it? I think to get away with four out of five is pretty good batting. When they were considering the speeding summons I thought you were well on the way to a six-month disqualification. Here you are, on the other hand, with one month only. This is still not very good but better than two and a half years, which is what it might have been."

Laurie Driver was staggered. He had not appreciated that two and a half years was even a possibility. It made one month sound almost welcome.

"I've got to agree, Mr. Care, that you have done a great job. I didn't realise I was facing two and a half years disqualification. To be honest I did feel that I was probably going to be disqualified anyway. In fact, I couldn't see any way out of it. One month's disqualification; that is almost nothing really, is it? At the same time I'm worried about my job. I suppose some people will say that I should have thought about it before and not feel sorry for myself afterwards. Still, that's my worry. I'd like to shake hands with you before I go. Just one more thing – can I ask you whether we can do anything about it, and possibly get my licence back before the month if things are really tough?"

"No, there is no chance of that at all Mr. Driver. In fact, you can't apply for a removal of a disqualification which is for less than a period of two years in length. Even then the period upon which you can apply for a removal of a disqualification differs according to the length of the disqualification. For example, if you were disqualified for three years you could apply for your licence back after two years. The periods are laid down in the Road Traffic Act. I don't know if you are interested but if you were disqualified for six months, six months, six months, six months and six months consecutively that adds up to two and a half years in total. Nevertheless, they are all separate six-month disqualifications. Once one appreciates that it is really five separate periods of six months then clearly you can't apply for your licence back at all. Two years plus is the minimum disqualification before you can think about getting a disqualification removed.

"Perhaps you would give some thought as to whether or not you wish to appeal against the disqualification. The most important consideration at this stage is whether or not you are going to lose your job. If the firm decides to sack you then I think we might lodge a notice of appeal. We can then make application to the magistrates to suspend your disqualification pending appeal. I think we will be able to persuade them to do that, particularly because of the short period of disqualification.

"If it is necessary to appeal then I have got to serve notice in writing upon the clerk to the justices. I've also got to serve notice on the person whose name appeared on your summons as the informant. We don't have all that much time. Can I suggest that you have a word with your employers when you go back to work. Try to get a decision out of them as quickly as possible as to whether they are going to keep you on at work. If they are going to sack you then ask them if they can leave their final decision until they hear from me. I will get the notice of appeal lodged, that is if you want to appeal, and I will apply for the disqualification to be suspended."

Laurie Driver looked at Mr. Care and said, "Well, I don't really feel in the mood to appeal at the moment because I suppose it will all be more cost."

Mr. Care said, "Well, yes, it might be. We could possibly get a further legal aid order for the purpose of the appeal. You've been on legal aid up to now so there is a strong possibility that you could have it extended. I agree that doesn't mean to say that you might not be ordered to pay a fairly high contribution towards the costs of the appeal even if your appeal is successful. It could, therefore, be a reasonably costly business. On the other hand, it might be worth it. It depends basically upon whether you are going to lose your job or not. Don't forget, however, that it isn't only a question of losing your job, it is also a question, with the unemployment situation being as it is, of when you are going to get another one. You really must weigh the cost of being unemployed against the cost of the appeal.

"I think we can leave it there now. I think it will be sufficient for me to say that the appeal lies to the Crown Court which is obviously a higher court than this. It will go before a Crown Court judge. He is a professional lawyer. Usually there will be lay justices sitting with him. The Crown Court might or might not be sympathetic. I can go as far as to make one comment. If you are sacked you have probably got nothing to lose.

"I think that's about all. Oh no, perhaps I can add that if it had been a 'Not guilty' plea we could also have appealed against the conviction. It would then have been a complete re-hearing. It would be as if it had never been heard at all. Where you are appealing against conviction all the witnesses can be called before the Crown Court and again it is as if they had never been called at the magistrates' court at all. The whole thing starts from the very beginning.

"In your case, however, we changed our plea to one of 'Guilty' so our appeal lies against sentence and the disqualification, unless you think the fine is excessive. I can tell you it's average for this court. If you appeal there don't seem to be any complications.

"Well that really is it, Mr. Driver. Just take care of yourself. Let me know as soon as possible whether or not you do wish to appeal against the disqualification. Don't forget what I've said. My advice is to appeal only if you lose your job but it's your decision.

"Incidentally, it has just occurred to me that the court didn't make any order for you to pay any contribution towards the legal aid, so that you will be getting your down payment back. I suspect that they didn't order it because they felt that you were perfectly justified in pursuing your

'Not guilty' plea in respect of the other matters. They could have ordered you to make a contribution even though the case had been dismissed, so that you are really very fortunate.

"You can offset the £15 you get back against the fine. You're even better off than you thought in the first place. The clerk to the court, or rather to be absolutely correct the clerk to the justices, will be sending the £15 in due course. If you don't hear from him then you should write and ask when you're going to receive it.

"Well, cheerio, Mr. Driver. Good luck with your employers."

Laurie Driver shook Mr. Care's hand and said, "I really would like to thank you. I don't really want to appeal but if it is a question of losing my job then I will, so I might be in touch with you. Thanks again."

Driver watched Mr. Care walking down the corridor and thought to himself, "Well, it was a good job the Union put me on to him."

CHAPTER 3

To appeal or not to appeal

Solicitor and client looked at each other in silence for a few moments. They had already followed the usual courtesies and Laurie Driver had explained that he had been sent back by his employers to see Mr. Care. They had asked him to tell Mr. Care that they were not going to sack him, but they still thought that he should consider appealing because of the problems he might face in the future due to the entry on his driving licence. His employers had made the point to him that if he was stopped again for any endorsable offence then he was probably going to be off the road for a minimum period of six months, and they would not be able to keep him on if that happened.

Mr. Care gave the matter some thought. "The situation is this, Mr. Driver. Of course we'll appeal if that is your wish. I'll take the necessary instructions from you. If after we've discussed the matter in a little more detail you are still of the same opinion, then I must advise you that I think this is a proper case for us to consider instructing counsel. I'm sure that you should have a barrister represent you at the Crown Court if you pursue your appeal. Technically I'm entitled to act for you at the hearing of the appeal. I nevertheless think it would be wise to have a barrister in this particular case. Before we discuss that let us decide whether or not you really should appeal.

"Your employers have a very good point. It did go through my mind to mention it to you when I was talking to you at court. Nevertheless, it's not always wise to appeal just for the sake of appealing. The Crown Court do have power to vary the magistrates' order and they might vary it in a way that is unacceptable to you. We are talking about an appeal against sentence and disqualification only. I explained to you when we met in the office that you won't be able to appeal against conviction because you changed your plea in court from one of 'Not guilty' to one of 'Guilty'. I still think it was wise to throw in the towel, as it were, and change your plea. Having done so – what now? Fortunately you've come to see me within the twenty-one day limit so we've got time to serve the necessary notices upon the clerk to the justices and upon the informant. That, however, is the least of our worries. Let me hear from you as to why you personally feel you should appeal and then I'll discuss the matter further."

Laurie Driver was a little bit puzzled by this approach. He had believed that all he needed to do was to instruct his solicitor to appeal and that would be that. He thought for a moment.

"Well, I think the only reason why I want to appeal is because of the fact that a month's disqualification on my licence is such a serious matter to me as a driver. I would like to have the disqualification removed. An endorsement is bad enough but an endorsement coupled with a disqualification is even worse. I also feel I'm bound to be disqualified for at least six months if I do anything while these endorsements are on my licence. I suppose that's it, Mr. Care. There is another point that I want to mention in just a minute but I think what I've said up to now explains why I want to appeal."

Mr. Care nodded.

"Yes, I can well understand your feelings. Quite frankly I still think that, on balance, you should let the whole thing rest. The evidence concerning the insurance, 'careless driving' and 'failing to stop' summonses will not be brought out in any appeal concerned with the speeding and, therefore, the problem that faces you stems from the fact that the magistrates did mitigate. Furthermore they mitigated a long way down the scale. Add to that the fact that your employers have decided not to sack you – you won't lose your job. I think the Crown Court will almost certainly come to the conclusion that any appeal is a lost cause. If you would like me to take counsel's opinion then I'll do so, or alternatively if you disagree with me then I will pursue the appeal for you. I've given you my opinion and despite my apparent youth I can tell you that it's an opinion based upon experience in such matters over the last few years. Of course, I might be wrong. After all the Crown Court's there for the purpose of hearing appeals. What do you really think?"

Laurie Driver was a little nonplussed. On the one hand his employers had told him to appeal. On the other hand his solicitor said he should not. He gave the whole matter some more thought and then spoke.

"Well, quite honestly I agree with you. It was only because my employers sent me in to ask about an appeal that I came at all. I don't think they really want me to appeal. They are thinking of me rather than themselves. I can straighten it out with them when I get back. I'll take your advice and we'll leave the question of appeal alone.

"Can I now mention the other point I wanted to raise? When I was stopped at the time by the policeman he gave me what he called a notice of intended prosecution. In the trade they're called 'nips' or N.I.P.s. But I've got it with me here and all it says on it is that I'm being reported for the possibility of prosecution for 'reckless driving', 'careless driving' and 'driving without reasonable consideration'. It doesn't mention speeding at all. I recollect reading, or hearing, about speeding being one of those offences where you have to receive a notice about prosecution, or at least to have a summons served on you within a particular time. What do you think?"

Mr. Care smiled.

"What you are saying is only the same as I've heard time and time again. There's a lot of confusion as to when the police need to warn the motorist about possible prosecution. I think I can help you most by explaining to you in some detail what's supposed to happen in these cases. It isn't easy to give you a short answer but I'll try to paint a general picture so that you will know what the situation is for the future.

"In simple terms, the Road Traffic Act requires that for

certain offences. 'Careless driving', 'reckless driving', 'driving without reasonable consideration' and speeding are four examples of offences in respect of which the police have to warn you that they are prosecuting you for committing an offence. There are others. Generally speaking if they don't warn you then you can't be convicted of the offence if you take objection to the proceedings at court. There are two or three very important points to note. One exception to the warning requirement is where a summons is served upon you within fourteen days of the commission of the offence.

"Another alternative is where a notice of intended prosecution is served upon you within fourteen days of the commission of the offence setting out the nature of the alleged offence, the time and the date and the place where the offence was committed. In some cases this can be served upon the registered owner of the vehicle – where the identity of the driver is not known. They can send the notice to you by post – which means registered post, or recorded delivery. Either is valid service as long as they send it to you at your last known address. Even if it's then returned to the police marked 'gone away', or if for some other reason it's not delivered, it is still good service.

"Another more common method of warning you as to intended prosecution is for the police to warn you at the scene of the incident of the intention to prosecute you for the alleged offence. The law goes on to say that courts must act as if the law in respect of N.I.P.s has been complied with unless the contrary is proved. This means, in effect, that it is up to you, in court, to object to the prosecution being brought on the ground that you hadn't received the necessary notice of intended prosecution.

"There are special provisions about prosecutions upon indictment. The word 'indictment' is, for your information, a technical term relating to offences tried at the Crown Court. One final and very important exception to the giving of a notice or a warning as to possible prosecution is that where there has been an accident, no matter how trivial, a notice of intended prosecution is *not* required.

"That's really what it's all about. There are four basic situations. Firstly, they can warn you at the time; secondly, if they don't warn you at the time they can send you a notice of intended prosecution (within fourteen days of the commission of the offence) by recorded delivery or by registered post to your last known address; thirdly, if they don't send a notice of intended prosecution they can serve a summons upon you within fourteen days of the commission of the offence; finally, where there has been an accident, a notice of intended prosecution is not necessary. Nevertheless, the court must assume that all that has to be done has been done, unless there is an objection taken in court.

"I didn't object – why? There are two very good reasons. The first is that there was at the very least an allegation of an accident, and the second is that there is the point I have also mentioned, which is that it is quite sufficient if the policeman makes it clear to you at the time why he stopped you and that he intends to report you. Words such as he used to you at the scene, to the effect that you were going faster than the permitted limit, would be sufficient. I think he used the expression, 'you were clocking it a bit'. That's quite enough for you to know that the policeman was alleging you had been speeding. He went on to say he would tell his senior officers about it and they would make up their minds whether to prosecute and that's a sufficient notice. In other words, he warned you at the time!

"Incidentally, the fact that you appeared at court and no objection was taken would have been sufficient to put the matter right. The law is well settled in that you can waive the need for a notice of intended prosecution by not objecting. Not that it would have made any difference in your case if I had objected. There was a warning given to you by the policeman and that complies with the law.

"Sorry to have taken so long to explain the position, but I hope that it will at least be helpful."

Laurie Driver had sat listening patiently to his solicitor.

"I am extremely grateful to you for the trouble you've taken, not only in court but out of court, to explain the law to me. I didn't really expect you to take so much trouble. I suppose you'll take it in the right way when I say that I hope we don't meet again. At the same time I would like to say thanks. I'd rather keep out of your way because if we meet it probably means that I'm in some more sort of trouble. If I am then I'll come and see you. You might like to know that I got the £15 back from the court. It seems a funny sort of procedure but I must say that I was pleased to receive it. Thanks again."

Mr. Care and Mr. Driver shook hands. Whether they would meet again in the future, only time would tell. There were still many miles left in the motoring life of Laurie Driver, once his right to drive had been restored to him.

Part II

LEGAL PROCEDURES IN ROAD TRAFFIC CASES

CHAPTER 4

The drinking driver

Space does not permit this important area of the law to be dealt with in any depth, but the subject is so important to all sections of the motoring public that mention of the subject must be made.

It is necessary to refer in some detail to the statutory provisions contained in the Road Traffic Act 1972. This Act sets out the several offences involved: driving or attempting to drive, and being in charge of motor vehicles with more than 80 milligrams of alcohol per 100 millilitres of blood, or more than 107 milligrams of alcohol per 100 millilitres of urine; the offence of failing, without reasonable excuse, to provide a specimen of blood or urine for a laboratory test after arrest; and that of failing or refusing to take a breath test on the approved breathalyser. Set out below are the relevant sections.

EXTRACT FROM ROAD TRAFFIC ACT 1972

SECTION 5 Driving or being in charge, when under influence of drink or drugs.

5. (1) A person who, when driving or attempting to drive a motor vehicle on a road or other public place, is unfit to drive through drink or drugs shall be guilty of an offence.

(2) Without prejudice to subsection (1) above, a person who, when in charge of a motor vehicle which is on a road or other public place, is unfit to drive through drink or drugs shall be guilty of an offence.

(3) For the purposes of subsection (2) above a person shall be deemed not to have been in charge of a motor vehicle if he proves that at the material time the circumstances were such that there was no likelihood of his driving it so long as he remained unfit to drive through drink or drugs.

(4) For the purposes of this section a person shall be taken to be unfit to drive if his ability to drive properly is for the time being impaired.

(5) A constable may arrest without warrant a person committing an offence under this section.

SECTION 6
Driving, or being in charge, with blood-alcohol concentration above the prescribed limit.

6. (1) If a person drives or attempts to drive a motor vehicle on a road or other public place, having consumed alcohol in such a quantity that the proportion thereof in his blood, as ascertained from a laboratory test for which he subsequently provides a specimen under section 9 of this Act, exceeds the prescribed limit at the time he provides the specimen, he shall be guilty of an offence.

(2) Without prejudice to subsection (1) above, if a person is in charge of a motor vehicle on a road or other public place having consumed alcohol as aforesaid, he shall be guilty of an offence.

(3) A person shall not be convicted under this section of being in charge of a motor vehicle if he proves that at the material time the circumstances were such that there was no likelihood of his driving it so long as there was any probability of his having alcohol in his blood in a proportion exceeding the prescribed limit.

(4) In determining for the purposes of subsection (3) above the likelihood of a person's driving a motor vehicle when he is injured or the vehicle is damaged, the jury, in the case of proceedings on indictment, may be directed to disregard, and the court in any other case may disregard, the fact that he had been injured or that the vehicle had been damaged.

SECTION 7
Evidence on charge of unfitness to drive.

7. (1) In any proceedings for an offence under section 5 of this Act, the court shall, subject to section 10(5) thereof, have regard to any evidence which may be given of the proportion or quantity of alcohol or of any drug which was contained in the blood or present in the body of the accused, as ascertained by analysis

of a specimen of blood taken from him with his consent by a medical practitioner, or of urine provided by him, at any material time; and if it is proved that the accused, when so requested by a constable at any such time, refused to consent to the taking of or to provide a specimen for analysis, his refusal may, unless reasonable cause therefor is shown, be treated as supporting any evidence given on behalf of the prosecution, or as rebutting any evidence given on behalf of the defence, with respect to his condition at that time.

(2) A person shall not be treated for the purposes of subsection (1) above as refusing to provide a specimen unless–

(a) he is first requested to provide a specimen of blood, but refuses to do so;

(b) he is then requested to provide two specimens of urine within one hour of the request, but fails to provide them within the hour or refuses at any time within the hour to provide them; and

(c) he is again requested to provide a specimen of blood, but refuses to do so.

(3) The first specimen of urine provided in pursuance of a request under subsection (2)*(b)* above shall be disregarded for the purposes of subsection (1) above.

SECTION 8
Breath tests.

8.–(1) A constable in uniform may require any person driving or attempting to drive a motor vehicle on a road or other public place to provide a specimen of breath for a breath test there or nearby, if the constable has reasonable cause–

(a) to suspect him of having alcohol in his body, or

(b) to suspect him of having committed a traffic offence while the vehicle was in motion;

but no requirement may be made by virtue of paragraph *(b)* above unless it is made as soon as reasonably practicable after the commission of the traffic offence.

(2) If an accident occurs owing to the presence of a motor vehicle on a road or other public place, a constable in uniform may require any person who he has reasonable cause to believe was driving or attempting to drive the vehicle at the time of the accident to

provide a specimen of breath for a breath test—

(*a*) except while that person is at a hospital as a patient, either at or near the place where the requirement is made or, if the constable thinks fit, at a police station specified by the constable;

(*b*) in the said excepted case, at the hospital;

but a person shall not be required to provide such a specimen while at a hospital as a patient if the medical practitioner in immediate charge of his case is not first notified of the proposal to make the requirement or objects to the provision of a specimen on the ground that its provision or the requirement to provide it would be prejudicial to the proper care or treatment of the patient.

(3) A person who, without reasonable excuse, fails to provide a specimen of breath for a breath test under subsection (1) or (2) above shall be guilty of an offence.

(4) If it appears to a constable in consequence of a breath test carried out by him on any person under subsection (1) or (2) above that the device by means of which the test is carried out indicates that the proportion of alcohol in that person's blood exceeds the prescribed limit, the constable may arrest that person without warrant except while that person is at a hospital as a patient.

(5) If a person required by a constable under subsection (1) or (2) above to provide a specimen of breath for a breath test fails to do so and the constable has reasonable cause to suspect him of having alcohol in his body, the constable may arrest him without warrant except while he is at a hospital as a patient.

(6) Subsections (4) and (5) above shall not be construed as prejudicing the provisions of section 5(5) of this Act.

(7) A person arrested under this section, or under the said section 5(5), shall, while at a police station, be given an opportunity to provide a specimen of breath for a breath test there.

(8) In this section "traffic offence" means an offence under any provision of this Act except Part V therof or under any provision of Part III of the Road
1960 c. 16 Traffic Act 1960 or the Road Traffic Regulation Act
1967 c. 76 1967.

SECTION 9
Laboratory tests.

9.—(1) A person who has been arrested under section 5(5) or 8 of this Act may, while at a police station, be required by a constable to provide a specimen for a laboratory test (which may be a specimen of blood or of urine), if he has previously been given an opportunity to provide a specimen of breath for a breath test at that station under subsection (7) of the said section 8, and either—

(*a*) it appears to a constable in consequence of the breath test that the device by means of which the test is carried out indicates that the proportion of alcohol in his blood exceeds the prescribed limit, or

(*b*) when given the opportunity to provide that specimen, he fails to do so.

(2) A person while at a hospital as a patient may be required by a constable to provide at the hospital a specimen for a laboratory test—

(*a*) if it apppears to a constable in consequence of a breath test carried out on that person under section 8(2) of this Act that the device by means of which the test is carried out indicates that the proportion of alcohol in his blood exceeds the prescribed limit, or

(*b*) if that person has been required, whether at the hospital or elsewhere, to provide a specimen of breath for a breath test, but fails to do so and a constable has reasonable cause to suspect him of having alcohol in his body;

but a person shall not be required to provide a specimen for a laboratory test under this subsection if the medical practitioner in immediate charge of his case is not first notified of the proposal to made the requirement or objects to the provision of a specimen on the ground that its provision, the requirement to provide it or a warning under subsection (7) below would be prejudicial to the proper care or treatment of the patient.

(3) A person who, without reasonable excuse, fails to provide a specimen for a laboratory test in pursuance of a requirement imposed under this section shall be guilty of an offence.

(4) Nothing in the foregoing provisions of this

section shall affect the provisions of section 7(1) of this Act.

(5) A person shall not be treated for the purposes of subsection (3) above as failing to provide a specimen unless—

(a) he is first requested to provide a specimen of blood, but refuses to do so;

(b) he is then requested to provide two specimens of urine within one hour of the request, but fails to provide them within the hour or refuses at any time within the hour to provide them; and

(c) he is again requested to provide a specimen of blood, but refuses to do so.

(6) The first specimen of urine provided in pursuance of a request under subsection (5)*(b)* above shall be disregarded for the purposes of section 6 of this Act.

(7) A constable shall on requiring any person under this section to provide a specimen for a laboratory test warn him that failure to provide a specimen of blood or urine may make him liable to imprisonment, a fine and disqualification, and, if the constable fails to do so, the court before which that person is charged with an offence under section 6 of this Act or this section may direct an acquittal or dismiss the charge, as the case may require.

In this subsection "disqualification" means disqualification for holding or obtaining a licence to drive a motor vehicle granted under Part III of this Act.

SECTION 10
Ancillary provisions as to evidence in proceedings for an offence under s. 5 or 6.

10.—(1) For the purposes of any proceedings for an offence under section 5 or 6 of this Act, a certificate purporting to be signed by an authorised analyst, and certifying—

(a) the proportion of alcohol or any drug found in a specimen identified by the certificate, and

(b) for the purposes only of proceedings for an offence under the said section 5, in the case of a specimen of urine, the proportion of alcohol or of that drug in the blood which corresponds to the proportion found in the specimen,

shall, subject to subsection (3) below, be evidence of the

matters so certified and of the qualification of the analyst.

(2) For the purposes of any proceedings for an offence under the said section 5 or 6, a certificate purporting to be signed by a medical practitioner that he took a specimen of blood from a person with his consent shall, subject to subsection (3) below, be evidence of the matters so certified and of the qualification of the medical practitioner.

(3) Subsections (1) and (2) above shall not apply to a certificate tendered on behalf of the prosecution unless a copy has been served on the accused not less than seven days before the hearing or trial, nor if the accused, not less than three days before the hearing or trial, or within such further time as the court may in special circumstances allow, has served notice on the prosecutor requiring the attendance at the hearing or trial of the person by whom the certificate was signed.

A copy of a certificate required by this subsection to be served on the accused or of a notice required by this subsection to be served on the prosecutor may either be personally served on the accused or the prosecutor (as the case may be) or sent to him by registered post or the recorded delivery service.

(4) In any proceedings in Scotland for an offence under the said section 5 or 6, a certificate complying with subsection (1) or (2) above and, where the person by whom such a certificate was signed is called as a witness, the evidence of that person, shall be sufficient evidence of the facts stated in the certificate.

(5) Where in proceedings for an offence under the said section 5 or 6 the accused, at the time a specimen of blood or urine was taken from or provided by him, asked to be supplied with such a specimen, evidence of the proportion of alcohol or any drug found in the specimen shall not be admissible on behalf of the prosecution unless—

(a) the specimen is either one of two taken or provided on the same occasion or is part of a single specimen which was divided into two parts at the time it was taken or provided, and

(b) the other specimen or part was supplied to the accused.

(6) A constable requesting any person to consent to the taking of or to provide a specimen of blood or urine for analysis shall offer to supply him, in a suitable container, part of the specimen or, in the case of a specimen of blood which it is not practicable to divide, another specimen which he may consent to have taken.

(7) In this section "authorised analyst" means any person possessing the qualifications prescribed by regulations made under section 89 of the Food and Drugs Act 1955, or section 27 of the Food and Drugs (Scotland) Act 1956, as qualifying persons for appointment as public analysts under those Acts, and any other person authorised by the Secretary of State to make analyses for the purposes of this section.

1955 c. 16
1956 c. 30

SECTION 11
Detention of persons while affected by alcohol.

11. Any person required to provide a specimen for a laboratory test under section 9(1) of this Act may thereafter be detained at the police station until he provides a specimen of breath for a breath test and it appears to a constable that the device by means of which the test is carried out indicates that the proportion of alcohol in that person's blood does not exceed the prescribed limit.

IMPLICATIONS OF THE ROAD TRAFFIC ACT 1972 (ss. 5–11)

By way of opening comments it should be observed that section 5 of the Act is now rarely used in practice by the police and this is partly because of the ease with which evidence can be obtained in excess alcohol (breathalyser) cases. Section 5, it will be noted, deals with a motorist brought before the court for driving (or attempting to drive) or being in charge of a motor vehicle on a road or other public place when unfit to drive through drink or drugs.

Prior to the Road Safety Act 1967 (it was in 1967 that the breathalyser was introduced), driving under the influence of alcohol and drunk in charge were the motoring/alcohol offences. It was because of the difficulty in securing convictions under that Act (presumably because of a "There go I but for the grace of God" attitude on the part of the jury) that the law relating to the breathalyser was introduced. Nevertheless, section 5 is still there to be used and from time to time it is. There are situations where the section 5 "driving under the influence" charge is more appropriate than the use of the breathalyser provisions. An example is where a motorist is stopped by the police because of the manner of his driving and then subsequently ceases to be a driver of a motor vehicle because he has been arrested, or similarly detained, so as to allow him to argue that driving has indeed ended.

In such cases he still leaves himself open to arrest for the offence of driving under the influence, provided there is evidence as to the manner of his driving, etc., and subsequent evidence that he was under the influence of drink or drugs. It is also interesting to note that following arrest under section 5 for driving under the influence the motorist can subsequently be requested at the police station to take a breath test. If the test is positive the police can then opt, if necessary, to proceed under the excess alcohol provisions, should the subsequent laboratory test supply the necessary evidence.

The advantage to the prosecution of the sections dealing with the breathalyser and laboratory tests is that there must be an automatic conviction provided that the necessary preliminary steps have been followed prior to the taking of a laboratory specimen and the analysis shows that the driver was above the specified limit at the time that he provided the specimen. In addition, there must also be an automatic conviction if, having been properly arrested under one or more of the sections set out above, he refuses to supply a specimen of blood or urine for analysis without reasonable excuse. It should be noted that whilst the refusal to supply a breath test can result in a fine, a refusal to supply a specimen of blood or urine can result in a "driver" being compulsorily disqualified, even if he can satisfy the court that he had not been drinking. He would also, of course, have to suffer the other penalties as provided by the law.

Automatic conviction

It seems sensible to list the necessary preliminary steps and conditions which will result in an automatic conviction.

(1) There must be a valid arrest of the "driver" either under section 5 of the Road Traffic Act 1972 (driving or being in charge of a motor vehicle when on a road or other public place when unfit to drive through drink or drugs), or under section 8 of the Road Traffic Act 1972 (which relates to breath tests, or the refusal or failure to provide a specimen of breath for a test).

(2) Once there has been a valid arrest under the Road Traffic Act, it is then necessary to prove that:

(a) the defendant was a driver of a motor vehicle (or was attempting to drive) when he was required to take a breath test and that the requirement was made because he was suspected of having an excess of alcohol in his body, or alternatively, he was suspected of having committed a moving road traffic offence;

or

(b) the motorist has been involved in a road traffic accident.

In both cases the breath test must have proved to be positive in order for an arrest to take place, or alternatively the motorist must have failed or refused to supply a breath test upon a proper request.

(3) Assuming a breath test has been positive, or there has been a failure or refusal followed by an arrest at the police station, there must be an offer of another breath test (that would apply where the defendant had been arrested under section 5, or under section 8). The second breath test must also be positive if the matter is to proceed further, or alternatively there must be a further refusal or a failure to supply such a test.

(4) The police must then require the arrested motorist to supply a specimen of blood or urine for the purpose of laboratory analysis and then must warn him of the consequences of refusal. Section 9 requires:

(a) that the motorist should be first requested to supply a specimen of blood;

(b) that if he refuses to supply a specimen of blood (which must be taken by a medical practitioner) he must then be requested to supply two specimens of urine within one hour of the request;

(c) that if he fails to provide the two specimens of urine within the hour, or refuses at *any time* within the hour to provide them, then he must be again requested to provide a specimen of blood. If he refuses this final request then automatic conviction will follow. If, on the other hand, he complies with the section and a specimen is taken he will be convicted only if the subsequent analysis proves him to be over the limit. The warning by the constable to the motorist about the consequences of failure or refusal to supply blood or urine must be to the effect that such a failure may render the motorist liable to imprisonment, a fine and disqualification.

(5) There are special provisions covering the situation where the specimen is to be taken from hospital patients and those provisions are set out in section 9 of the Act.

LOOPHOLES IN THE ROAD TRAFFIC ACT 1972

Much has been said in the past about the various loopholes in the Road Traffic Act concerning excess alcohol cases, but these have slowly and surely been closed. The major gap in the law was concerned with whether or not the motorist required to take a breath test was still a driver. The other major loophole revolves around what is now called the "hip flask" defence. I will now deal with these two matters in brief.

The "driver" defence

The words "driving" or "attempting to drive", which are contained in section 8 of the Road Traffic Act 1972, have caused difficulty. It is important to note, right from the beginning, that breath tests do not apply to a person who is in charge of a motor vehicle. The breath test can only be required where a person is driving or attempting to drive a motor vehicle on a road, and the constable who is requiring a specimen of breath suspects the driver of having alcohol in his body, or suspects him of having committed a traffic offence whilst the vehicle was in motion. From this section springs the roadside test situation.

There is also, of course, the possibility of a breath test being administered following a road traffic accident. This occurs where the constable has reasonable cause to believe that the person whom he requires to take a breath test was the driver or was attempting to drive the vehicle at the time of the accident. There are also provisions in accident cases for taking a breath test at the hospital. We are, therefore, dealing with the words "driving" or "attempting to drive".

There have been many cases on this particular point but in 1973 an appeal came before the Queen's Bench Division. There was a five judge court and the reserved judgment summarises the collective effect of what had previously been irreconcilable decisions. The case is *Edkins* v. *Knowles* [1973] 2 All E.R., page 503. It is also reported in 137 J.P at page 550. The facts of the case are quite interesting.

At about 11.00 p.m. two plain clothes officers in a police car saw the defendant driving fast and erratically. They followed him for about three miles to a disused holiday camp where he was living. As they followed the defendant's car they sent out a wireless call requesting the attendance of a traffic patrol car. They did not attempt to overtake and stop the defendant because they thought it would be too dangerous. The defendant finally stopped his motor vehicle in the holiday camp when they drew up beside him, identified themselves and asked him to await the arrival of a traffic patrol car. The defendant did so and remained seated in his car. About five minutes later the traffic patrol car arrived with uniformed officers.

A plain clothes officer then brought the defendant over to the traffic patrol car and in the presence of the defendant told the uniformed officer how the defendant's vehicle had been driven. The uniformed officer noticed that the defendant's breath smelt of alcohol and as a result of what he had been told and what he had smelt he asked for a breath test. This proved to be positive. The defendant was arrested and after the prescribed testing procedure was followed it revealed that his urine contained 174 milligrams of alcohol in 100 millilitres of urine, which was well above the prescribed limit.

At the magistrates' court the defendant did not give evidence. It was submitted, on his behalf, that he had no case to answer on the ground that the uniformed policeman had no right to require him to take a breath test. He submitted to the court two points. Firstly, that the breath specimen had not been requested nearby a road or other public place, but that submission was rejected; secondly, that he could not have been lawfully required to take a breath test as he had ceased driving before the constable in uniform had reasonable grounds to suspect him of having alcohol in his body, or of having committed a moving road traffic offence. From the appeal several points were settled.

Firstly, whether a motorist is driving at the relevant time is a question of fact to be determined by the justices, directing themselves to the same considerations as a judge would direct a jury in his summing up. There had been several decisions as to what these considerations should be, but the collective effect of the decisions may be summarised as follows.

(1) The vehicle does not have to be in motion; there will always be a brief interval of time after the vehicle has been brought to rest and before the motorist has completed those operations necessarily connected with driving, such as applying the handbrake, switching off the ignition and securing the vehicle, during which he must still be considered to be driving.

(2) When a motorist stops before he has completed his journey he may still be driving; an obvious example is when he is halted at traffic lights. Each case will depend on its own facts, but generally the following questions will be relevant. *(a)* What was the purpose of the stop? If it is connected with the driving, and not for some purpose unconnected with the driving, the facts may justify a finding that the driving is continuing although the vehicle is stationary. *(b)* For how long did he stop? The longer he stops the more difficult

it becomes to regard him as still driving. *(c)* Did he get out of the vehicle? If he remains in the vehicle it is some indication, though not a conclusive one, that he is still driving.

(3) If a motorist is stopped by a constable in uniform who immediately forms the suspicion that the motorist has alcohol in his body, the motorist should be regarded as still driving at the moment when the suspicion is formed: but if an appreciable time elapses before the constable's suspicion is aroused, it will be a question of fact and degree as to whether the motorist is still to be considered as driving at that time.

(4) When a motorist has arrived at the end of his journey then subject to the brief interval referred to in *(a)* above he can no longer he regarded as driving.

(5) When a motorist has been effectively prevented or persuaded from driving, he can no longer be considered to be driving.

Returning now to the present case, the magistrates held that the uniformed officer was not entitled to require a breath test and they dismissed the information. The Divisional Court held that the magistrates were right to do so. The constable was only entitled to require a test if he had reasonable grounds for suspicion under section 2(1)*(a)* or *(b)* of the Act at a time when the respondent was driving. In fact, he did not form his suspicion until about five minutes after the respondent had reached the end of his journey and at a time when he was effectively prevented from driving by the plain clothes officers. On these facts the justices rightly concluded that the defendant was not driving when first suspected by the uniformed officer. The appeal was, therefore, dismissed.

This, of course, still leaves us with several situations where there is a huge area of doubt as to when a person is or is not driving. It is submitted that if he leaves his car for a temporary purpose, for example to clean his headlights or to go to the toilet, then if he intends to resume driving without any significant delay he is still the driver. On the other hand, a person who has finished his journey and has left and locked up his car can no longer be the driver. He might also cease to be the driver because he is effectively prevented from continuing on his journey by reason of having been arrested by the police in respect of some other matter. Having once been arrested then his driving has ended.

Clearly, therefore, it is essentially a question of fact; but in the case of a defendant who has left his motor vehicle the reason for stopping and the length of time that elapses from the moment the driver leaves his motor vehicle to the moment when he is spoken to by the police is obviously an important factor. It does not necessarily follow, of course, that because the driver has managed to reach his home he is no longer the driver, because of a doctrine which can be called "in hot pursuit".

This means that provided there is a continuous course of action on the part of the police between the pursuit and the eventual requirement of the driver to take a breath test then he can still, in proper cases, be held to be the driver even though his physical driving of the motor vehicle has ceased and even though he has reached the apparent safety of his own home. It depends, therefore, purely on the facts of the individual case, but if the defendant can satisfy the court that he was no longer a driver of a motor vehicle when required to take a breath test then he cannot be convicted of an offence under those particular provisions.

In appropriate cases he can still be proceeded against under section 5 of the Road Traffic Act for driving or attempting to drive a motor vehicle when under the influence of drink or drugs. Indeed he could still be arrested for that particular offence and subsequently required to take a breath test at the police station.

In the vast majority of cases, however, the attention of the police has been drawn to the motor vehicle because of some reason unconnected with the manner of the defendant's driving. A typical example is where the attention of the police is drawn to the vehicle because the rear lights are not properly illuminated. In such a case the motorist will still be able to avoid the normal consequences of driving with an excess of alcohol in his blood if he can satisfy the court that he was not the driver of a motor vehicle when required to take a breath test by the uniformed police officer. The word "uniformed" is relevant because of the fact that it has been held that a plain clothes officer cannot require the breath test to be taken.

The "hip flask" defence

The second major area of difficulty is, or has been, called the "hip flask" defence. These cases arise as a result of a not uncommon situation where the motorist has actually ended his driving of the vehicle but is still legally the driver. In some cases he has temporarily ended his driving for purposes similar to those which have already been outlined. Nevertheless, being the driver he then consumes intoxicating liquor. Sometimes this will indeed be from a hip flask. On other occasions – such as in "hot pursuit" cases – he has managed to reach his home and then takes a drink of whisky or some other similar intoxicating liquor in order to "steady his nerves". The result of the consumption of this intoxicating liquor is that he cannot then be properly breathalysed. This is because any subsequent analysis of the amount of intoxicating liquor in his body will include a proportion of intoxicating liquor which has entered his body *after* he had been driving a motor vehicle on a road.

The breathalyser provisions only apply where the analysis relates to the amount of intoxicating liquor in his body at the time he was driving and the subsequent consumption of alcohol prevents the breathalyser provisions form applying. If a motorist deliberately takes a drink of intoxicating liquor in order to avoid the consequences of the breathalyser law then he could, if necessary, be prosecuted for wilfully obstructing the police in the execution of their duty.

That deals, in brief, with two of the major problems which have arisen as a result of prosecutions under the breathalyser laws. Clearly, the police will still proceed under this particular Act as often as they are able because if all the various points are able to be proved by the prosecution then a conviction is certain. Once the proper procedure has been followed then on the whole it becomes a matter of medical evidence, which cannot generally be contradicted. Of course, the two areas which have been discussed show that there is still room for argument as to the facts and as to whether or not the police officer was justified in commencing procedure in the first place. Nevertheless, the law concerning breathalyser offences is sufficiently certain to ensure that the breathalyser will be used in preference to prosecutions under section 5 which deals with driving under the influence of drink or drugs.

Before moving on to section 5 it is worth noting, once again, that the breathalyser provisions, as they relate to roadside tests, apply only to a motorist who is driving or attempting to drive a motor vehicle with an excess of alcohol in his blood or urine above the prescribed limit. What then if a motorist is in charge? The answer lies in sections 5 and 6 of the Road Traffic Act 1972.

Section 6(2) specifically makes it an offence to be in charge of a motor vehicle with a blood/alcohol concentration which is above the prescribed limit. It is possible that a motorist might be arrested as a driver following a roadside test and subsequently be charged with the offence of "being in charge" rather than driving or attempting to drive. The more usual situation, however, is following a straightforward arrest for being in charge of a motor vehicle in contravention of section 5 or section 6.

It might be that after arrest the motorist is asked to consent to a laboratory test. Consent is, of course, always a prerequisite to the taking of a specimen of blood or urine. It follows, therefore, that the warning as to refusal must always be given if such a request is made. If there is a failure or refusal after the warning then the penalties, as provided by the Road Traffic Act, will automatically follow, unless there can be proved to be sufficient reason to justify such failure or refusal. If a motorist is found by a police constable apparently in charge of a motor vehicle and the constable forms the opinion that he has consumed alcohol then a decision can be made to arrest under section 5(5). He must be given the opportunity, at the station, to provide a breath test under s.8(7). If this is positive or if he fails to provide one he can be required to provide a specimen for a laboratory test under s.9(1). If the test is negative and there is sufficient evidence to proceed on s.5(2) (unfit to drive) a specimen may be requested under s.7.

If arrested for being in charge of a motor vehicle when under the influence of drink or drugs, or being in charge with a blood/alcohol concentration above the prescribed limit, the motorist has a statutory defence if he can prove that at the material time the circumstances were such that there was no likelihood of his driving so long as there was any probability of his having alcohol in his blood in excess of the prescribed limit if charged under section 6, or alternatively, that there was no likelihood of his driving so long as he remained unfit to drive through drink or drugs if charged under section 5. It is submitted that there is always the possibility that a person with less than the prescribed limit could be convicted under section 5 of the Act (if charged under that section) because the standard of proof to justify a conviction is that he shall be taken to be unfit to drive if his ability to drive properly is, for the time being, impaired.

SUMMARY

The following points are worth noting.

Excess alcohol

(1) A constable can require any motorist whom he reasonably suspects of driving or attempting to drive a motor vehicle with an excess of alcohol in his blood above the prescribed limit to take a breath test.

(2) The constable must be acting in good faith.

(3) He must use an approved device (at present the Alcotest R 80).

(4) The constable must follow the prescribed procedure in administering the breath test.

(5) If the test is positive he must arrest the motorist.

(6) There must be a proper and lawful arrest, otherwise what follows subsequently is not lawful.

(7) At the police station the motorist must be offered the opportunity to take a second breath test.

(8) If he fails or refuses or if the second breath test is positive, then he must be asked to consent to a specimen of

blood being taken for the purposes of a laboratory test. He must be given a statutory warning as to the consequences of failure to provide a specimen.

(9) The specimen of blood must be taken by a registered medical practitioner.

(10) The provision of a specimen of urine would follow a request for a specimen of blood and a refusal to supply such a specimen. There must, by law, be provided two specimens of urine within one hour of the request of the supply. Failure or refusal to supply such a specimen results in –

(11) A further request to supply a specimen of blood.

(12) Failure or refusal to supply either a specimen of blood or a specimen of urine results in automatic conviction, unless the motorist can satisfy the court that he has a reasonable excuse.

Driving under the influence of alcohol

(13) A person arrested for driving or attempting to drive under the influence of alcohol can subsequently be given the opportunity to take a breath test at a police station and, upon failure or refusal to supply a breath test or upon a positive reading, can be required to supply a specimen of blood or urine for a laboratory test as described above.

In charge of a motor vehicle when under the influence of drink or drugs and excess alcohol cases

(14) The offending motorist can be asked to consent to the supply of a specimen of blood or urine and the consequences of failure or refusal are as above.

Accidents

(15) A motorist is subject to the special provisions of the section as set out in the text of this book following a road traffic accident when driving a motor vehicle, etc. If he is a hospital patient then the constable must comply with the detailed prcedure as set out in the section, which involves obtaining certain consents from the hospital doctor up to and including the point of discharge from hospital as a patient.

Except where the motorist is prosecuted for being in charge of a motor vehicle, where he is convicted under section 5 or section 6 of the Road Traffic Act 1972, he faces compulsory disqualification, unless he can satisfy the court that there are special reasons to avoid the normal consequences of the penalty. Special reasons must be circumstances peculiar to the commission of the offence and not to the offender (*see* Chapter 5).

CHAPTER 5

Endorsement and disqualification

I: Relevant offences

Our unhappy motorist has now reached the stage where his original shock, or his anger, at being accused of a road traffic offence has abated. He still, nevertheless, remembers that his worry was whether or not the offence he has committed would render him liable to have his licence endorsed, or to being disqualified, or, of course, to both. He is now aware that in the case of a limited number of offences concerning his tyres, steering and brakes, etc., he can avoid endorsement if he can satisfy the court that he did not know, or did not have any reasonable cause to suspect, that the defect existed. He is still far from certain as to where to find the answer concerning other road traffic offences, that is the answer to whether endorsement will follow. In fact, he need only refer to the Schedule which follows, listing the sections referring to the relevant offences and their penalties, in order to find the answer, not only to whether his licence will be endorsed but also to whether the matter can only be dealt with at magistrates' court level, or whether there is an option for it to be dealt with by a higher court (the Crown Court).

The first column contains the section of the particular Act which creates the offence and one must always be prepared to refer to that section. What is also extremely valuable about the Schedule is that it sets out, in the clearest possible terms, the maximum punishment the court can impose, whether or not the offence is endorsable and whether or not the offender is liable to disqualification. There is also an appropriate note against those offences relating to steering, tyres and brakes where there is a statutory answer provided to compulsory endorsement.

ROAD TRAFFIC ACT 1972

PART IV. – Road Traffic

SCHEDULE 4

(as amended by the Heavy Commercial Vehicles (Controls and Regulations) Act 1973, the Road Traffic Act 1974, the Road Traffic (Drivers' Ages and Hours of Work) Act 1976, Scheds. 1 and 3, the Secretary of State for Transport Order 1976, S.1. 1976 No. 1775, the Criminal Law Act 1977, s. 28 and Scheds. 1, 5, 6, 12 and 13 and the Transport Act 1978, Sched. 3.)

Sections 93, 101, 177, 179, 180, 181, 183.

PROSECUTION AND PUNISHMENT OF OFFENCES

PART I

Offences under this Act

1 Provision creating offence	2 General nature of offence	3 Mode of prosecution	4 Punishment	5 Disqualification	6 Endorsement	7 Additional provisions
1	Causing death by reckless driving.	On indictment.	5 years or, in the case of a conviction by a court in Scotland other than the High Court of Judiciary, 2 years.	Obligatory.	Obligatory.	Section 181 and paragraph 3 of Part IV of this Schedule apply.

2	Reckless driving.	(a) Summarily.	6 months or the prescribed sum (within the meaning of s.28 of the Criminal Law Act 1977) [£1,000] or both.	(a) Obligatory, if committed within 3 years after a previous conviction of an offence under section 1 or 2.	Obligatory.	Sections 179, 181 and 183 and paragraphs 1, 2, 3, 5, and 6 of Part IV of this Schedule apply.
		(b) On indictment.	2 years or a fine or both	(b) Discretionary if committed otherwise than as mentioned in paragraph (a) above.		
3	Careless, and inconsiderate driving.	Summarily.	£500	Discretionary.	Obligatory.	Sections 179, 181 and 183 and paragraphs 3A, 4, 5 and 7 of Part IV of this Schedule apply.
5(1)	Driving or attempting to drive when unfit to drive through drink or drugs.	Summarily.	6 months or £1,000 or both.	Obligatory.	Obligatory.	Sections 181 and 183 and paragraph 3 of Part IV of this Schedule apply.
5(2)	Being in charge of a motor vehicle when unfit to drive through drink or drugs.	Summarily.	3 months or £500 or both	Discretionary.	Obligatory.	Sections 181 and 183 and paragraph 3 of Part IV of this Schedule apply.
6(1)	Driving or attempting to drive with blood-alcohol concentration above the prescribed limit.	Summarily.	6 months or £1,000 or both.	Obligatory.	Obligatory.	Sections 181 and 183 and paragraph 3 of Part IV of this Schedule apply.

1 Provision creating offence	2 General nature of offence	3 Mode of prosecution	4 Punishment	5 Disqualification	6 Endorsement	7 Additional provisions
6(2)	Being in charge of a motor vehicle with blood-alcohol concentration above the prescribed limit.	Summarily.	3 months or £500 or both.	Discretionary.	Obligatory.	Sections 181 and 183 and paragraph 3 of Part IV of this Schedule apply.
8(3)	Failing to provide a specimen of breath for a breath test.	Summarily.	£50	—	—	Sections 181 and 183 apply.
9(3)	Failing to provide a specimen of blood or urine for a laboratory test.	Summarily.	(i) Where it is shown that at the relevant time (as defined in Part V of this Schedule) the offender was driving or attempting to drive a motor vehicle on a road or other public place, 6 months or £1,000 or both. (ii) Where in any other case it is shown that at that time the offender was in charge of a motor vehicle on a road or other public place, 3 months or £500 or both.	(a) Obligatory if it is shown as mentioned in paragraph (i) of column 4. (b) Discretionary if it is not so shown.	Obligatory.	Sections 181 and 183 and paragraph 3 of Part IV of this Schedule apply.

14	Motor racing and speed trials on highways.	Summarily.	£200.	Obligatory.	Obligatory	Sections 181 and 183 apply.
15	Other unauthorised or irregular competitions or trials on highways.	Summarily.	£100.	–	–	–
16	Carrying passenger on motor-cycle contrary to section 16.	Summarily.	£50	Discretionary.	Obligatory.	Sections 181 and 183 apply.
17	Reckless cycling	Summarily.	£50.	–	–	Sections 179, 181 and 183 apply.
18	Careless, and inconsiderate cycling.	Summarily.	£20.	–	–	Sections 179, 181 and 183 and paragraphs 3A, 4 and 7 of Part IV of this Schedule apply.
19	Cycling when unfit through drink or drugs.	Summarily.	£50.	–	–	Sections 181 and 183 apply.
20	Unauthorised or irregular cycle racing or trials of speed on highways.	Summarily.	£20.	–	–	Sections 181 and 183 apply.
21	Carrying passenger on bicycle contrary to section 21.	Summarily.	£20.	–	–	Sections 181 and 183 apply.

1 Provision creating offence	2 General nature of offence	3 Mode of prosecution	4 Punishment	5 Disqualification	6 Endorsement	7 Additional provisions
22	Failing to comply with traffic directions.	Summarily.	£100.	Discretionary, if committed in respect of a motor vehicle by a failure to comply with a direction of a constable or an indication given by a sign specified for the purposes of this paragraph in regulations made by the Secretary of State for Transport, the Secretary of State for Wales and the Secretary of State for Scotland acting jointly.	Obligatory. if committed as described in the entry in column 5 relating to offence.	Sections 179, 181 and 183 apply.
23	Pedestrian failing to stop when directed by constable regulating traffic.	Summarily.	£50	—	—	—
24	Leaving vehicles in dangerous positions.	Summarily.	£100	Discretionary, if committed in respect of a motor vehicle.	Obligatory, if committed in respect of a motor vehicle.	Sections 179, 181 and 183 apply.

25(4)	Failing to stop after accident and give particulars or report accident.	Summarily.	£100.	Discretionary.	Obligatory.	Sections 181 and 183 apply.
26(2)	Obstructing inspection of vehicles after accident.	Summarily.	£50.	–	–	–
29	Tampering with motor vehicles.	Summarily.	£100.	–	–	Section 181 applies.
30(1)	Holding or getting on to vehicle in order to be carried.	Summarily.	£20.	–	–	Section 181 applies.
30(2)	Holding on to vehicle in order to be towed.	Summarily.	£20.	–	–	Sections 181 and 183 apply.
31(1)	Dogs on designated roads without being held on a lead.	Summarily.	£20.	–	–	–
32(3)	Driving or riding motor cycles in contravention of regulations requiring wearing of protective headgear.	Summarily.	£50	–	–	–

1 Provision creating offence	2 General nature of offence	3 Mode of prosecution	4 Punishment	5 Disqualification	6 Endorsement	7 Additional provisions
33	Selling, etc., helmet not of prescribed type as helmet for affording protection for motor cyclists.	Summarily.	£100.	—	—	—
34(4)	Causing, etc. heavy motor vehicles to be driven or to haul without proper crew.	Summarily.	£100.	—	—	Section 181 applies.
35(3)	Unauthorised motor vehicle trial on footpaths or bridleways.	Summarily	£100.	—	—	Sections 181 and 183 apply.
36	Driving motor vehicles elsewhere than on roads.	Summarily.	£20.	—	—	Sections 181 and 183 apply.
36A	Prohibition of parking of heavy commercial vehicles on verges and footways.	Summarily.	£100.	—	—	Sections. 181 and 183 apply.

36B	Prohibition of parking of vehicles on verges, central reservations and footways.	Summarily.	£100.	–	–	Sections 181 and 183 apply.
40 (5)	Contravention of construction and use regulations.	Summarily.	£400 in the case of an offence of using or causing or permitting the use of, a goods vehicle – *(a)* so as to cause, or to be likely to cause, danger by the condition of the vehicle or its parts or accessories, the number of passengers carried by it, or the weight, distribution, packing or adjustment of its load; or *(b)* in breach of a construction and use requirement as to brakes, steering-gear, tyres or any description of weight, or	Discretionary if committed by using, or causing or permitting the use of, any motor vehicle or trailer – *(a)* as described in paragraph *(a)* or paragraph *(c)* in the entry in column 4 relating to this offence; or *(b)* in breach of a construction and use requirement as to brakes, steering-gear, or tyres; except where the offender proves that he did not know and had no reasonable cause to suspect that the facts of the case were such that the offence would be committed.	Obligatory if committed as described in the entry in column 5 relating to this offence, but subject to the exception there mentioned.	Sections 181 and 183 apply.

1 Provision creating offence	2 General nature of offence	3 Mode of prosecution	4 Punishment	5 Disqualification	6 Endorsement	7 Additional provisions
40 (5) (*contd.*)			(*c*) for any purpose for which it is so unsuitable as to cause or to be likely to cause danger; £400 in the case of an offence of carrying on a goods vehicle a load which, by reason of its in security or position, is likely to cause danger; £100 in any other case.	Discretionary if committed by carrying on a motor vehicle or trailer a load which, by reason of its insecurity or position, is likely to cause danger, but subject to the exception above.		
44 (1)	Using, etc., vehicle without required test certificate being in force.	Summarily.	£100.	—	—	Sections 181 and 183 apply.

Regulations under 45 (7)	Contravention of requirement of regulations that driver of goods vehicle being tested be present throughout test or drive vehicle, etc., which is declared by regulations to be an offence.	Summarily.	£100.	—	—	Sections 181 and 183 apply.
46 (1)	Using, etc., goods vehicle without required plating certificate being in force.	Summarily.	£100	—	—	Sections 181 and 183 apply.
46 (2)	Using, etc., goods vehicle without required goods vehicle test certificate being in force.	Summarily	£200.	—	—	—
46 (3)	Using, etc., goods vehicle with alteration thereto required to be but not notified to Secretary of State under regulations under section 45.	Summarily.	£100.	—	—	Sections 181 and 183 apply.

1 Provision creating offence	2 General nature of offence	3 Mode of prosecution	4 Punishment	5 Disqualification	6 Endorsement	7 Additional provisions
Regulations under 50 (5)	Contravention of requirement of regulations that driver of goods vehicle being tested after notifiable alteration be present throughout test and drive vehicle, etc., which is declared by regulations to be an offence.	Summarily.	£100.	–	–	Sections 181 and 183 apply.
51 (1)	Using, etc., . . . vehicle without required certificate being in force showing that it complies with type approval requirements applicable to it.	Summarily.	£100.	–	–	Sections 181 and 183 apply.

51 (2)	Using, etc., certain . . . vehicles for drawing trailer when plating certificate does not specify maximum laden weight for vehicle and trailer.	Summarily.	£50.	—	—	Sections 181 and 183 apply.
51 (3)	Using, etc., . . . vehicle with alteration thereto required to be but not notified to Secretary of State under regulations under section 48.	Summarily.	£100.	—	—	Sections 181 and 183 apply.
53 (4)	Obstructing testing of vehicle by examiner on road or failing to comply with requirements of section 53 or Schedule 3.	Summarily.	£50.	—	—	—

1 Provision creating offence	2 General nature of offence	3 Mode of prosecution	4 Punishment	5 Disqualification	6 Endorsement	7 Additional provisions
54 (5) (including application by 55 (3))	Failure of owner of vehicle discovered to be defective on roadside test or further test to give required certificate or declaration.	Summarily.	£50.	—	—	—
54 (6) (including application by 55 (3))	Failure of person in charge of vehicle on roadside test or further test to give particulars of owner.	Summarily	£50.	—	—	—
55 (5)	Obstructing further testing of vehicle by Secretary of State's officer or failing to comply with requirements of section 55 or paragraph 3 or of Schedule 3.	Summarily.	£50.	—	—	—

56 (3)	Obstructing goods vehicle examiner inspecting goods vehicle or entering premises where such vehicle believed to be.	Summarily.	£50.	—	—	—
56 (5)	Person in charge of stationary goods vehicle refusing etc., to proceed to nearby place of inspection.	Summarily.	£50.	—	—	—
57 (9)	Driving, etc., goods vehicle in contravention of prohibition on driving it as being unfit for service or refusing, neglecting or otherwise failing to comply with a direction to remove a dangerous heavy commercial vehicle.	Summarily.	£400.	—	—	Sections 181 and 183 apply.

1 Provision creating offence	2 General nature of offence	3 Mode of prosecution	4 Punishment	5 Disqualification	6 Endorsement	7 Additional provisions
59 (3)	Contravention of regulations requiring goods vehicle operator to inspect, and keep records of inspections of, goods vehicles.	Summarily.	£100.	—	—	—
60 (3)	Selling, etc., unroadworthy vehicle or trailer or altering vehicle or trailer so as to make it unroadworthy.	Summarily.	£200.	—	—	—
60A (1)	Fitting of defec- or unsuitable vehicle parts.	Summarily.	£200.	—	—	—
60A (3)	Selling defective or unsuitable vehicle parts.	Summarily.	£200.	—	—	—

60A (6)	Obstructing examiner testing vehicles to ascertain whether defective or unsuitable part has been fitted, etc.	Summarily.	£100.	—	—	—
61 (2)	Obstructing examiner testing condition of used vehicles at sale rooms, etc.	Summarily.	£50.	—	—	—
62	Selling, etc., goods vehicle without required certificate being in force showing that it complies with type approval requirements applicable to it.	Summarily.	£200.	—	—	—
66 (5)	Selling, etc., pedal cycle in contravention of regulations as to brakes, bells, etc.	Summarily.	£100.	—	—	—

1 Provision creating offence	2 General nature of offence	3 Mode of prosecution	4 Punishment	5 Disqualification	6 Endorsement	7 Additional provisions
81 (1)	Causing, etc., vehicle to be on road in contravention of provisions as to lighting, etc., of vehicles.	Summarily.	£100.	–	–	Sections 181 and 183 apply.
81 (2)	Selling, etc., wrongly made tail lamps or reflectors.	Summarily.	£50.	–	–	–
84 (1)	Driving without a licence.	Summarily.	£100.	Discretionary, if the offence is committed by driving a motor vehicle in a case where either no licence authorising the driving of that vehicle could have been granted to the offender or, if a provisional (but no other) licence to drive it could have been granted to him, the driving would not have complied with the conditions thereof.	Obligatory, if committed as described in the entry in column 5 relating to this offence.	Sections 181 and 183 apply.

84 (2)	Causing or permitting a person to drive without a licence.	Summarily.	£100.	—	—	Section 181 applies.
88 (6)	Failing to comply with any conditions prescribed for driving under provisional licence or full licence treated as provisional licence.	Summarily.	£100.	Discretionary.	Obligatory.	Sections 181 and 183 apply.
89 (3)	Driving licence holder failing, when his particulars become incorrect, to surrender licence and give particulars.	Summarily.	£50.	—	—	Section 180 applies.
91 (1)	Driving with uncorrected defective eyesight.	Summarily.	£100.	Discretionary.	Obligatory.	—
91 (2)	Refusing to submit to test of eyesight.	Summarily.	£100.	Discretionary.	Obligatory.	—
99 (a)	Obtaining driving licence while disqualified.	Summarily.	£100.	—	—	Section 180 applies.
99 (b)	Driving while disqualified.	(a) Summarily.	6 months or the prescribed sum (within the meaning of s.28 of the Criminal Law Act 1977) [£1,000] , or both.	Discretionary.	Obligatory.	Sections 180, 181 and 183 apply.

1 Provision creating offence	2 General nature of offence	3 Mode of prosecution	4 Punishment	5 Disqualification	6 Endorsement	7 Additional provisions
99 (b) cont.		(b) On indictment	12 months or a fine or both.			
101 (4) (including application by 103 (4))	Failing to produce licence to court for endorsement on conviction of offence involving obligatory endorsement or on committal for sentence, etc., for offence involving obligatory or discretionary disqualification when no interim disqualification ordered.	Summarily.	£100.	–	–	–
101 (6)	Applying for or obtaining licence without giving particulars of current endorsement.	Summarily.	£100.	–	–	–
103 (2)	Failing to produce driving licence to	Summarily.	£100.	–	–	–

	court making order for interim disqualification on committal for sentence etc.					
104 (4)	Failing to state to court or give information as to date of birth or sex.	Summarily.	£50	—	—	—
104 (5)	Failing to furnish Secretary of State with evidence of date of birth etc.	Summarily.	£50.	—	—	—
111 (2)	Failing to produce to court Northern Ireland driving licence.	Summarily.	£100.	—	—	
112 (1)	Driving heavy goods vehicle without heavy goods vehicle driver's licence.	Summarily.	£100.	—	—	Sections 181 and 183 apply.
112 (2)	Causing or permitting a person to drive heavy goods vehicle without heavy goods vehicle driver's licence.	Summarily.	£100.	—	—	Section 181 applies.
114 (3)	Failing to comply	Summarily.	£100.	—	—	Sections 181 and 183 apply.

1 Provision creating offence	2 General nature of offence	3 Mode of prosecution	4 Punishment	5 Disqualification	6 Endorsement	7 Additional provisions
	with conditions of heavy goods vehicle driver's licence.					
114 (4)	Causing or permitting a person under 21 to drive heavy goods vehicle in contravention of conditions of heavy goods vehicle driver's licence.	Summarily.	£100.	—	—	Section 181 applies.
Regulations under 119 (2)	Contravention of regulations about heavy goods vehicle driver's licences which is declared by regulation to be an offence.	Summarily.	£50.	—	—	—
126 (3)	Giving of paid driving instruction by unregistered and unlicensed persons or their employers.	Summarily.	£200.	—	—	—

135 (2)	Unregistered instructors using title or displaying badge, etc., prescribed for registered instructors, and employers using title, etc., in relation to his unregistered instructor or issuing misleading advertisement, etc.	Summarily.	£200.	—	—	—
136	Failure of instructor to surrender to Registrar certificate or licence.	Summarily.	£50.	—	—	—
137 (3)	Failing to produce certificate of registration or licence as driving instructor.	Summarily.	£50.	—	—	—
143	Using motor vehicle while uninsured or unsecured against third-party risks.	Summarily.	£200.	Discretionary.	Obligatory.	Sections 180, 181 and 183 apply
147 (4)	Failing to surrender certificate of insurance or	Summarily.	£50.	—	—	—

1 Provision creating offence	2 General nature of offence	3 Mode of prosecution	4 Punishment	5 Disqualification	6 Endorsement	7 Additional provisions
	security to insurer on cancellation or make statutory declaration of loss or destruction.					
151 (2)	Failing to give information, or wilfully making false statement, as to insurance or security when claim made.	Summarily.	£200.	–	–	–
159	Failing to stop vehicle when required by constable.	Summarily.	£100.	–	–	Sections 181 and 183 apply.
160 (1)	Refusing or neglecting to allow motor vehicle or trailer to be weighed, etc.	Summarily.	£400.	–	–	Sections 181 and 183 apply.
161 (4)	Failing to produce driving licence to constable or to state date of birth.	Summarily.	£50.	–	–	Sections 181 and 183 apply.

161 (5)	Failing to furnish Secretary of State with evidence of date of birth, etc.	Summarily.	£50.	—	—	—
162 (1)	Failing to give constable certain names and addresses or to produce certificate of insurance or certain test and other like certificates.	Summarily.	£50.	—	—	Sections 181 and 183 apply.
162 (3)	Supervisor of learner-driver failing to give constable certain names and addresses.	Summarily.	£50.	—	—	Section 181 applies.
164 (1)	Refusing to give, or giving false, name and address in case of reckless, dangerous, careless or inconsiderate driving or cycling.	Summarily.	£100.	—	—	Sections 181 and 183 apply.
165	Pedestrian failing to give constable his name and address after failing to stop when directed by constable controlling traffic.	Summarily.	£20.	—	—	—

1 Provision creating offence	2 General nature of offence	3 Mode of prosecution	4 Punishment	5 Disqualification	6 Endorsement	7 Additional provisions
166 (1)	Failure by driver, in case of accident involving injury to another, to produce evidence of insurance or security or to report accident.	Summarily.	£100.	—	—	Sections 181 and 183 apply.
167	Failure by owner of motor vehicle to give police information for verifying compliance with requirement of compulsory insurance or security.	Summarily.	£200.	—	—	Sections 181 and 183 apply.
168 (3)	Failure of person keeping vehicle and others to give police information as to identity of driver, etc., in the case of certain offences.	Summarily.	£50.	—	—	—
169 (1)	Forgery, etc., of licences, test certificates, certificates	(a) Summarily. (b) On indictment.	£200. 2 years.	—	—	Section 180 applies.

	of insurance and other documents and things.					
170 (1)	Making false statements in connection with licences under this Act and with registration as an approved driving instructor.	Summarily.	£200.	—	—	Section 180 applies.
170 (2)	Making or making use of, false statements relating to goods vehicles.	Summarily.	£200.	—	—	—
170 (3)	Producing false evidence or making false declaration in connection with applications for vehicle excise licences for vehicles required to have test certificates.	Summarily.	£200.	—	—	—
170 (4)	Making false statements as to the remedying of defects discovered in vehicles on roadside tests.	Summarily.	£200.	—	—	—

1 Provision creating offence	2 General nature of offence	3 Mode of prosecution	4 Punishment	5 Disqualification	6 Endorsement	7 Additional provisions
170 (5)	Making, or making use of, false entry in records required to be kept of condition of goods vehicles.	Summarily.	£200.	—	—	
170 (5A)	Failure to notify Secretary of State of onset of, or deterioration in, relevant or prospective disability.	Summarily.	£100.	—	—	Section 180 applies.
170 (6)	Making false statement or withholding material information in order to obtain the issue of insurance certificates, etc.	Summarily.	£200.	—	—	Section 180 applies.
171	Issuing false insurance certificates, etc., or false test certificates.	Summarily	£200.	—	—	Section 180 applies.
172	Using goods vehicle with unauthorised	Summarily.	£100.	—	—	

	weights as well as authorised weights marked thereon.					
174	Personation of, or of person employed by, authorised examiner.	Summarily.	£100.	–	–	–
175	Taking, etc., in Scotland a motor vehicle without authority or, knowing that it has been so taken, driving it or allowing oneself to be carried in it without authority.	(a) Summarily. (b) On indictment	3 months or £100 12 months or a fine or both.	Discretionary.	Obligatory.	Sections 181 and 183 and paragraph 8 of Part IV of this Schedule apply.
187 (2)	Failing to attend, give evidence or produce documents to, inquiry held by Secretary of State, etc.	Summarily.	£20	–	–	–
Schedule I para.5(1)	Applying warranty to protective helmet in defending proceed ings under section 33 where no warranty given.	Summarily.	£50.	–	–	–
para.5(2)	Giving to purchaser of protective helmet a false warranty in case where warranty might be defence in proceedings under section 33.	Summarily.	£50.	–	–	–

PART II

Other Offences Involving Obligatory Disqualification and Endorsement

Manslaughter or, in Scotland, culpable homicide by the driver of a motor vehicle.

PART III

Other Offences Involving Discretionary Disqualification and Obligatory Endorsement

1. Stealing or attempting to steal a motor vehicle.

2. An offence, or attempt to commit an offence, in respect of a motor vehicle under section 12 of the Theft Act 1968 (taking conveyance without consent of owner etc. or, knowing it has been so taken, driving it or allowing oneself to be carried in it).

1968 c. 60

3. An offence under section 25 of the Theft Act 1968 (going equipped for stealing, etc.) committed with reference to the theft or taking of motor vehicles.

4. An offence under section 13(4) of the Road Traffic Regulation Act 1967 (contravention of traffic regulations on special roads) committed in respect of a motor vehicle otherwise than by unlawfully stopping or allowing the vehicle to remain at rest on a part of a special road on which vehicles are in certain circumstances permitted to remain at rest.

1967 c. 76

5. An offence under section 23(5) of the Road Traffic Regulation Act 1967 (contravention of pedestrian crossing regulations) committed in respect of a motor vehicle.

6. An offence under section 25(2) of the Road Traffic Regulation Act 1967 (failure to

obey sign exhibited by school crossing patrol) committed in respect of a motor vehicle.

7. An offence under section 26(6) or 26A(5) of the Road Traffic Regulation Act 1967 (contravention of order prohibiting or restricting use of street playground by vehicles) committed in respect of a motor vehicle.

8. An offence punishable by virtue of section 78A of the Road Traffic Regulation Act 1967 (speeding offences under that and other Acts).

CHAPTER 6

Endorsement and disqualification

II: Methods of avoidance

PENALTIES: COMPULSORY AND AVOIDABLE

Introduction

The question that must enter the mind of every motorist, when stopped for a road traffic offence, is surely, "Will my licence have to be endorsed?" If the "unfortunate" motorist happens to have collected two previous endorsements he will then ask, "Will I be disqualified?" and also, "Can I avoid disqualification?"

Whether one can ever answer those questions satisfactorily depends upon many things, but in particular, it often rests upon the circumstances of the offence for which the motorist has been stopped and the nature of the offence. The nature of the offence might, in itself, indicate compulsory disqualification, unless special reasons can be advanced to the court. If it is an offence contained in the Schedule shown in an earlier chapter of this book (*see* pp. 92 to 121) then endorsement may automatically follow – unless once again special reasons are advanced and accepted by the court.

On the other hand, if one is asking a question about disqualification (rather than endorsement) then the first question to be asked and answered is, "Does the offence itself require that disqualification must be compulsory?" The second question might then well be, "In view of the fact that I have two endorsements on my licence already – will I have to suffer 'totting-up' disqualification?" The two questions are answered in different ways. The first is answered, "Yes, I can possibly avoid disqualification if I can place before the court evidence of special reasons, which means reasons special to the offence itself and not special to me as a driver or as a defendant." The second (which relates to "totting-up" disqualifications) can be answered, "Yes, I can avoid disqualification if the court accepts that I have mitigating circumstances." Mitigating circumstances can be anything that the court will accept as mitigating the normal consequences of conviction.

Compulsory disqualification

The following offences involve compulsory disqualification.

(1) Causing death by reckless driving.

(2) Reckless driving where there is an offence within previous three years, after a previous conviction for an offence under sections 1 or 2, i.e. causing death by reckless driving or careless driving.

(3) Driving (or attempting to drive) whilst unfit through the influence of drink or drugs.

(4) Driving (or attempting to drive) with an excessive amount of alcohol in the blood.

(5) Failing to provide a blood or urine specimen for laboratory testing, in cases where at the *relevant* time the offender was driving (or attempting to drive) a motor vehicle on a road in a public place, following:

(a) a requirement to take a breath test;

(b) an accident when driving a motor vehicle (if section 8(2) applies, at the time of the accident);

(c) arrest for being unfit to drive (or attempting to drive whilst unfit).

(6) Motor racing or speed trials on highways.

To avoid compulsory disqualification the motorist needs to advance special reasons to the court. Special reasons must be special to the offence itself and not to the offender. This will be explained in more detail.

Compulsory endorsement

Most of the offences which involve compulsory endorsement are shown in Schedule 4 to the Road Traffic Act 1972. Column 6 is the relevant column (*see* pp. 92 to 119). There are, however, eight other examples of offences involving discretionary disqualification and obligatory endorsement (these are shown on pp. 120-1).

Compulsory endorsement can only be avoided if special reasons are advanced and accepted. In this respect they are similar to compulsory disqualifications.

"Totting-up" disqualifications (third endorsement within three years)

At the risk of being repetitious, there now follows the text of section 93(3) of the Road Traffic Act 1972 which makes it clear what is meant in law by a "totting-up" disqualification.

> "Where a person convicted of an offence involving obligatory or discretionary disqualification has within the three years immediately preceding the commission of the offence been convicted on not less than two occasions of any such offence and particulars of the convictions have been ordered to be endorsed in accordance with section 101 of this Act, the court shall order him to be disqualified for such period not less than six months as the court thinks fit, unless the court is satisfied, having regard to all the circumstances, that there are grounds for mitigating the normal consequences of the conviction and thinks fit to order him to be disqualified for a shorter period or not to order him to be disqualified."

At first sight a "totting-up" disqualification is a compulsory disqualification. This is because the section says that a motorist liable to disqualification under that part of the section must be disqualified for *at least* six months.

It is the word "unless" which follows that gives the motorist additional hope in these matters. The reader will have noted the further words which clearly allow the court a discretion in such cases, provided it is satisfied that there are sufficient grounds to mitigate the normal consequences of conviction. If the court is so satisfied then it might – again at its own discretion – disqualify for a shorter period, or not disqualify at all, as it thinks fit. In arriving at this decision the court is further entitled to have regard to all the circumstances; this means the circumstances of the offence as well as the circumstances of the offender. The major difference between special reasons and mitigating circumstances is that is the case of special reasons only circumstances peculiar to the offence can be accepted by the court; whereas in the case of mitigating circumstances to avoid "totting-up" disqualification the court is entitled to consider the circumstances in their totality.

General considerations

There are, therefore, three situations as follows.

(1) Compulsory disqualification – by virtue of the offence (special reasons to avoid disqualification/endorsement).

(2) Scheduled offences involving compulsory endorsement (special reasons again required to avoid endorsement).

(3) "Totting-up" disqualification (the two previous endorsements situation) where mitigating circumstances can be accepted. These can relate either to the offence or to the offender.

Special reason and mitigating circumstances are dealt with below but it is perhaps pertinent to note the following additional points.

(1) If the offence is not shown in Schedule 4 to the Road Traffic Act 1972 (including Part III of that Schedule) as involving obligatory endorsement, it is *not* endorsable by a magistrates' court.

(2) If the offence is endorsable then disqualification can (in some cases must) be ordered.

(3) Except for "totting-up" disqualifications all endorsements and other disqualifications commence forthwith and run concurrently. "Totting-up" disqualifications always run consecutively to any other imposed on the same day, or to any other type of disqualification imposed previously.

(4) Whenever endorsement/disqualification can be ordered then the court can also disqualify the driver until he or she

passes a test. This type of disqualification can commence from the end of any other disqualification period.

(5) One must always note the special defence to endorsement allowed in respect of certain construction and use offences (i.e. brakes, tyres, steering, dangerous condition of vehicle and dangerous adjustment of load). The court does not need to endorse if satisfied that the offender did not know and had no reasonable cause to suspect that the facts of the case were such that the offence would be committed. (*See* pp. 99-100, columns 4 and 5 of Schedule 4).

(6) There is one example of a possible disqualification without endorsement – this is where the Crown Court disqualifies, upon indictment, an offender convicted of using a motor vehicle in furtherance of theft.

(7) Perhaps one should also note that in at least one case it is possible that a court is satisfied that a motorist has committed an offence and yet cannot order either endorsement or disqualification. This rare example is where the court proceeds to make a hospital order under the Mental Health Act 1960, because such an order does not rank as a conviction. On the other hand, an order placing a defendant on probation or an order of conditional discharge/absolute discharge does, for this limited purpose, rank as a conviction in that an endorsement must also be recorded in the absence of special reasons and it is possible that "totting-up" disqualification might also follow.

SPECIAL REASONS

Introduction

Special reasons have been the subject of a large number of judicial decisions. They must be circumstances special to the offence and not to the offender but the tests have been clearly defined. A case of *R.* v. *Wickins* (1958) 42 Cr. App. R. 236 laid down four criteria. They are as follows.

(1) It must be a mitigating or extenuating circumstance.

(2) It must not amount, in law, to a defence to the charge.

(3) It must be directly connected with the commission of the offence.

(4) The matter must be one the court ought properly to take into consideration when imposing punishment.

The tests (1), (2) and (4) can clearly also be considered as mitigating circumstances. Test (3) is, however, entirely on its own. It is exclusive to the definition of a special reason. The other three tests, it is suggested, are necessary because the relevant section states that the court "need not" endorse if it finds a special reason and thinks fit not to do so. It is, therefore, possible for a special reason to be advanced to the court and accepted as a special reason, and yet for the court still to endorse or disqualify if it thinks fit.

The four tests

It must be a mitigating or extenuating circumstance

Even if a fact can be put forward as a special reason and has been accepted in the past as such it does not follow that endorsement will not ensue. This was decided in the case of *Delaroy-Hall* v. *Tadman, Watson* v. *Last, Earl* v. *Lloyd* [1969] 1 All E.R. 25. In this particular case, with which I shall deal in more detail later, it was said that the slight degree of culpability involved did not amount to a special reason. Although of its type the facts just placed him in an "offence" category, an offence had been committed. Nevertheless, the normal consequences – endorsement, etc. – should follow. A special reason, in other words, must be found in something other than in the triviality of the offence itself.

Trivialities can, however, be troublesome. In careless driving and dangerous driving cases it seems clear that triviality cannot amount to a special reason (*Nicholson* v. *Brown* [1974] Crim. L. R. 187); therefore, the "small bump" cases must result in an endorsement. It appears that careless driving is careless driving, irrespective of degree. The situation is, however, less clear in excess alcohol cases. Let us, therefore, look at some examples.

In *James* v. *Hall* [1968] Crim. L. R. 507 the appellant was the father of a bride and guests were invited to his home for drinks. His car was in the roadway outside his drive. As the evening wore on he realised that he was "over the limit" as far as driving was concerned and rather than risk taking his car out he decided to park it in his garage for the night. Outside in the street was the representative of the law who saw the appellant get into his car and drive it the extremely short distance from where it was parked outside his house to his drive. One might be excused if one though – at first sight – that this was a sensible action. The appellant was, however, properly breathalysed and as a result arrested. He was subsequently convicted and disqualified. On appeal the Divisional Court held that the short distance he had driven from the road into his own drive was, in the special facts of the case, special to the offence and that all four tests applied to the case. The disqualification was quashed.

The short distance of driving is not, however, necessarily a special reason. A lorry driver was disqualified for driving only a short distance in order to park in a more suitable placc and his appeal was not successful (presumably because in his case there was a real possibility of him driving again whilst unfit).

Other short examples of what have been held to be special reasons include the following.

(1) An insurance case – where the defendant was misled by the action of another committing the offence.

(2) Where the defendant was legally liable but morally blameless (driver/employer relationships) such as described earlier in this book.

(3) Where the defendant was speeding to avoid delaying court business – a case which involved a solicitor's articled clerk (*Police Prosecutor* v. *Humphreys* [1970] Crim.L.R. 234).

There are, of course, many more but these might well suffice to prove the point that a special reason must involve a mitigating or extenuating circumstance.

It must not amount, in law, to a defence to the charge
This is a problem facing advocates from time to time. An example might be useful. At one court, recently, an advocate was representing a defendant who had pleaded guilty to having 319 milligrams of alcohol in his blood. The advocate asked the magistrates not to disqualify for longer than the minimum three-year period (it was his second offence in ten years) and attempted to put forward as a special reason for imposing *less* than the minimum three years' disqualification the fact that the defendant had had a couple of "scotches" in his home, after the accident but before the breathalyser was administered. As by that time he had *prima facie* ended his driving, advice was tendered to the magistrates by their clerk that not only could this not be accepted as a special reason but if the argument was to be pursued then a plea of "Not guilty" should be entered and the "Guilty" plea rejected. The advocate (apparently not having much faith in his client's instructions) tried to resist this by arguing that even if the defendant had had four whiskies his client would still have been well over the limit (indeed this might well have been true). This did not, however, impress the court because what he said, if subsequently believed, amounted to a defence to the charge. The important point was that it could not, therefore, amount to a special reason for endorsement or disqualification purposes.

Advocates should, of course, always bear in mind the vitally important provisions of column 5 in Schedule 4, which give exemption from endorsement for certain construction and use offences.

It must be directly connected with the offence (and not the offender)
A case dealing with this point is *R.* v. *Jackson* [1969] 2 All E.R. 453 (which reviewed the decision of *R.* v. *Wickins* (1958) which has been referred to earlier in this book). This was a Court of Appeal case. In the case of *Jackson* (after affirming the four specific principles) the Court of Appeal went on to make it clear that *special reasons which the court may take into account may well be different according to the offence committed.* The court especially distinguished excess alcohol from all other endorsable offences.

The matter must be one which the court ought properly to take into account when imposing punishment
To a certain extent this is an overlap with the first and second points but it stands on its own in that there are several examples of matters which are not taken into account when imposing punishment in certain cases, e.g. defendant's lack of intent in insurance and speeding cases, because of their absolute nature, although their reasons (rather than intentions) can and often are properly taken into account, e.g. emergency cases.

ACCEPTABILITY OF SPECIAL REASONS

In examining special reasons in the past the courts have made it abundantly clear that what is a special reason in one case might not be in another. They have laid down different standards in the cases of the following:

(1) dangerous driving (now reckless driving);
(2) drinking and driving;
(3) insurance cases;
(4) driving while disqualified.

It is clear from the decisions of the courts that special reasons differ according to the nature of the offence. This is perhaps as it should be, because a reason which is special to a person speeding to an emergency is perhaps understandably different to what is special if that person has an excess of alcohol in his blood, or drives dangerously. Let us, therefore, look at some of the different problems that have, from time to time, faced the courts.

Drinking and driving cases

This is, in itself, a difficult area of the law and it will be helpful if it is divided into different categories as follows.

Drink "lacing" cases
From time to time a defendant argues that his or her drink was "laced". Listed below are three of the more important cases on this point.

(1) The case of *Pugsley* v. *Hunter* [1973] 2 All E.R. 10

decided that the defendant must establish:

(a) that his drink was "laced";

(b) that he did not know or suspect that his drink was "laced";

(c) that if his drink had not been "laced" the alcohol level in his blood would not have exceeded the prescribed limit;

(d) that he must establish *(c)* by means of medical or scientific evidence; unless

(e) it is obvious to a layman that the added drink explains the excess.

(2) Another case of interest is *Alexander* v. *Latter* [1972] Crim. L.R. 646. In this case the Divisional Court upheld a finding that there were special reasons where a defendant had been offered diabetic lager as an alternative to ordinary lager. The barman did not inform the defendant that diabetic lager is much stronger than ordinary larger (in this case it was twice as strong).

On the other hand, the opposite was found in the case of *Adams* v. *Bradley* [1975] Crim. L.R. 168. In this second case the defendant drank strong lager without appreciating its strength. The difference clearly lies in the fact that in the case of *Alexander* v. *Latter* the defendant was misled, whereas in *Adams* v. *Bradley* the defendant himself chose the lager without making any enquiry.

(3) The third case is that of *R.* v. *Messom* [1973] R.T.R. 140. Here the defendant had asked for a large ginger ale together with a small whisky. He was given a small ginger ale topped up with a large brandy. This again was a classic example of a defendant being misled and special reasons were accepted.

Driving with excess of alcohol in the body

It is the reason for driving that is usually advanced as a special reason and, therefore, this category, in itself, can be subdivided. Firstly, there is the plea of sudden emergency. It is often argued before the court that an unexpected emergency arose. The question is, can this be accepted as a special reason? Let us look at some examples.

In the case of *Brown* v. *Dyerson* [1968] 3 All E.R. 39 the facts were that the defendant was convicted before Bow Street Magistrates' Court of an excess alcohol offence. The magistrates did not disqualify him, because of what they considered to be special reasons. There were that:

(*a*) a medical emergency had occurred; and
(*b*) his driving was not impaired.

As far as the second point was concerned the magistrates reached this conclusion on a statement volunteered by the prosecution, to the effect that there was no danger caused, or likely to be caused, by the respondent's driving and that his behaviour throughout was consistent with that of a normal man not impaired by drink. On appeal the Divisional Court said that whilst not arriving at a final conclusion on this matter this was not a case where the fact that the defendant's ability to drive was not impaired could constitute a special reason.

It was the "medical emergency" issue that was of particular interest. In respect of this point the Divisional Court said that there could, no doubt, be suitable cases where a medical emergency could constitute a special reason; if by "medical emergency" one means an unexpected situation arising in which a man who had been drinking but not intending to drive is impelled to drive a motor car by a sudden medical necessity.

In this case the driver of the car was driving a sick girl to her home. The sick girl was, in fact, the owner of the car. The magistrates' court had not been told the circumstances in which the girl became sick, or indeed the nature of the sickness, although it was accepted by the prosecution that she was ill. The Appeal Court had no difficulty in saying that the bare fact that the respondent was driving a sick girl home in her own motor car was hardly even a relevant mitigating circumstance, let alone a special reason for not disqualifying.

This case, therefore, makes it clear that a sudden, unexpected medical emergency might well – in proper cases

– amount to a special reason if the driver had not intended to drive prior to the emergency arising; but the nature of the emergency and the fact that it was unexpected are clearly matters upon which the court must be satisfied.

It was, conversely, held *not* to be a special reason in the following cases.

(1) In *R.* v. *Baines* [1970] Crim.L.R. 590 the defendant drove his car, at night, to rescue his partner's mother, who was stranded. Unfortunately, for him, it was noted that he could have explored other methods of transport – which he had not. It was held that there were no special reasons.

(2) Another example of this type of situation is found in the case of *Evans* v. *Bray* [1977] R.T.R. 24. In this case the defendant's wife had gone on holiday. She had forgotten tablets which she needed – she suffered from blood pressure. One can understand the action of the husband, who took the tablets to her by car. He had, however, been drinking and again it was said that his action was understandable but could not amount to a special reason. Clearly he could have, if necessary, contacted the emergency services, or alternatively, he could, presumably, have used other methods of transport.

Note that there is no special dispensation afforded to doctors, firemen, ambulance drivers and the like in emergency cases, because emergencies are their business and they should be used to dealing with them within the law. On the other hand, there is no reason why a court should not be sympathetic to a doctor, etc., if he is called to a sudden, unexpected disaster when otherwise not "on call".

Short distance of driving

Courts have shown a reluctance to establish any principle as to whether a short distance of driving can, or cannot, be a special reason.

(1) In *R.* v. *McIntyre* [1976] R.T.R. 330 the defendant genuinely belived he was being requested by a police officer to move his car. He drove it for a short distance so as to re-park it. There was no intention on his part otherwise to drive it home. This was subsequently held to be a special reason.

(2) In *James* v. *Hall* – which has been previously quoted – the short distance of driving was held to be an adequate special reason.

In each of these cases the important point to note is that there was no possibility of any danger being caused to any other road user. Whilst this is not the sole criteria it seems to have been an important factor when one looks at the converse decisions which are contained in the following cases.

(1) In *Coombs* v. *Kehoe* [1972] R.T.R. 224, magistrates who had acquitted a lorry driver were later directed to convict him in circumstances where he had driven 200 yards through a busy street in order to park his motor lorry in what he considered to be a safer position but collided with cars as he attempted to park.

(2) In the case of *R.* v. *Mullarkey* [1970] Crim. L.R. 406, a defendant who drove some 400 yards after midnight in winter when there was very little traffic about was, nevertheless, disqualified and it was held that these circumstances could not amount to special reasons.

Reckless and careless driving cases

The general comments which follow will include what is known to all motorists as the offence of dangerous driving.

Emergency cases

(1) In the case of *R.* v. *Lundt-Smith* [1964] 3 All E.R. 225, an ambulance driver crossed traffic lights on red. He was conveying an emergency case to hospital. So far as he was concerned, it was safe to cross the lights but, in fact, a motor cyclist was approaching and the collision which resulted was fatal. The motor cyclist was killed. The ambulance driver pleaded guilty to the offence (as it then was) of causing death by dangerous driving but in granting him an absolute discharge the judge also found that there were special reasons and did not disqualify him.

(2) A similar approach is to be found in the case of *Wood* v. *Richards* [1977] Crim. L.R. 295. In this case the magistrates convicted a police officer of careless driving when responding to an emergency call. They then went on to find

special reasons for not endorsing the police officer's licence. Both findings were upheld. It was said firstly that there were no special tests in these cases to be applied to police officers and secondly that, nevertheless, what occurred could amount to a special reason.

Triviality of offence
This problem has been considered by the courts from time to time. The following are perhaps indicative of the courts' general attitude.

(1) In *Nicholson* v. *Brown* [1974] R.T.R. 177 it was said that the proposition that if a man is guilty of careless driving he can be excused endorsement of his licence on the basis of special reasons merely because it was not a bad case is not acceptable. Similarly, it is not an acceptable proposition that he can be excused endorsement because the degree of blameworthiness was slight. The line to be drawn is that between guilt and innocence. If the defendant is guilty then the consequences of endorsement must follow, unless there is some special reason which can be properly treated as such (not such a matter as that the offence itself was not a serious one).

(2) Similarly, in *Delaroy-Hall* v. *Tadman; Watson* v. *Last; Earl* v. *Lloyd* [1969] 2 Q.B. 208 it was said that there were no special reasons in a case where the analysis of a defendant's blood-alcohol level was only just above the prescribed limit.

It would appear from these decisions that in order to satisfy the court that there are special reasons relating to the offence and not to the offender the court must be satisfied about matters other than the facts which constitute the offence itself. As far as endorsement/disqualification is concerned there would appear to be no degree of offence so as to excuse the natural consequences of conviction.

Speed limits

Emergency cases
Little point will be served by reiterating the specific and general points that have been discussed under the earlier

headings. It will suffice to note that special reasons can be found where a defendant exceeds a speed limit by reason of an emergency. An interesting example is provided by the case of *Police Prosecutor* v. *Humphreys* [1970] Crim. L.R. 234, where the Divisional Court refused to intervene when magistrates found special reasons in the fact that the defendant – a solicitor's articled clerk – was hurrying to Quarter Sessions in order to instruct counsel as to a matter before that court. The defendant had been held up on route for reasons beyond his control and he exceeded the speed limit in his anxiety that he should not hold up the business of the court. This is rather out of the ordinary in an example of an emergency case, and should be read as one which depended upon the special facts. One would usually be looking for the sudden and unexpected situation which, of necessity, would excuse a speed limit offence by reason of its being a true emergency.

Leaving to one side the statutory exemption to speeding which is afforded to police vehicles, etc. and the "emergency" case, exceeding the speed limit is an offence of such strict liability that it is difficult to envisage many situations where special reasons can be advanced which are acceptable to the court. So often the defendant attempts to argue reasons which relate to him as a driver (for example that an endorsement might affect his livelihood), but he is unable to advance any reasons special to the offence itself which would allow him to avoid the obligatory endorsement.

A good example of the strictness of liability in these matters is shown by the case of *Walker* v. *Rawlinson* [1976] R.T.R. 94, where it was said that ignorance on the part of the defendant that a 30 m.p.h. area is normally created by a system of street lighting with the lights placed not more than 200 yards apart cannot be a special reason. The fact is that he was in a restricted speed limit area – it was a built-up area – and whether he knew it or not was quite immaterial.

In another case it was held not to be a special reason that the defendant was last in line of a number of vehicles all travelling at 40 m.p.h. plus, and because of this the driver was under the misapprehension that he was in a 40 m.p.h.

limit. Again ignorance of the fact that he was in a built-up area was not taken to be a special reason as to why his licence should not be endorsed.

Reporting accidents

It is always possible that special reasons could be found where, for example, two drivers involved in a collision both agreed at the time that the accident was too trival to report, and did not therefore exchange names and addresses. If then one of the drivers does report the incident, special reasons in such circumstances might well be advanced and found.

Insurance

Defendant misled

The fact that the defendant was misled has been the subject of a number of appeals and it is clear that in proper cases this can amount to a special reason. There are a number of examples as follows.

(1) In *Lyons* v. *May* [1948] 2 All E.R. 1062 the owner of a motor lorry requested the proprietor of a garage to drive the motor vehicle from the garage to his own premises. He automatically assumed that the garage proprietor would be covered by his own insurance. He was not covered by insurance and did not inform the owner of the motor lorry that he was not covered. This was held to amount to a special reason.

(2) Another example is to be found in the case of *Labrum* v. *Williamson* [1947] 1 All E.R. 824. In this case application was made for full cover but the policy was issued for named drivers only. The difference was not pointed out by the insurance company and it was agreed that the policy holder had been misled. This was accepted as a special reason.

On the other hand, it was held in the case of *Swell* v. *McKechnie* (1956) Crim. L.R. 423 that in these matters ignorance of the law cannot be a special reason. In another case it was held that the fact that a defendant had made a number of attempts to obtain a policy of insurance and that he was not personally trying deliberately to evade the law was not a special reason.

Finally, it should be carefully noted that the defendant is under an obligation to satisfy the court that he was indeed misled. It is not sufficient to have, for example, an honest belief that he was covered by insurance which later proved to be groundless. The test is to ask whether he was misled rather than what he believed to be the position. This is not forgetting the statutory defence which can be put forward by an employee under section 143 of the Road Traffic Act 1972 where he can satisfy the court that he neither knew, nor had reason to believe, that there was not in force a policy of insurance (assuming that he was using the vehicle in the course of his employment and that the vehicle did not belong to him and was not in his possession under a contract of hiring or loan).

General considerations

(1) Traffic signs;
(2) pedestrian crossings;
(3) school crossings;
(4) construction and use regulations.

Triviality with regard to (1), (2) and (3)
It is unnecessary to repeat what has already been written on this matter, in that triviality will not amount, in itself, to a special reason (except in the very limited area of public policy). On the other hand, one can envisage a situation where, for example, traffic lights appear to be jammed. They are showing red in all directions and have been for some time. One could argue that there is a special reason if one proceeded slowly and with care. Another example might well be where a defendant proceeds against a red light because he is misled by the signal of a police officer. Nevertheless, the general rule must be that the offence is absolute in its nature and it is not easy to think of many examples where endorsement can be avoided.

Emergency cases with regard to (1), (2) and (3)
Emergency cases have been mentioned and clearly can amount to special reasons in proper circumstances. Similarly,

the fact that a defendant is entirely without fault might well amount to a special reason though the offence is itself absolute.

An example of this could be where someone jumps in the path of a car approaching a pedestrian crossing and the driver is unable to accord precedence. If no fault at all lies with the driver then there seems to be no reason why the court should not find special reasons.

Construction and use regulations

In dealing with construction and use matters one must constantly bear in mind the statutory defence to endorsement that has already been referred to on p. 126. In appropriate cases a driver can avoid endorsement (brakes, tyres, steering, etc.) where he can satisfy the court that he did not know the defect existed, or had no reasonable cause to suspect that it did. With this exception the problems facing motorists with regard to endorsable offences and special reasons also face the motorist who offends against the construction and use regulations (where compulsory endorsement is required by law). It might again be possible to satisfy the court that no fault of any sort lies with the driver; for example, where delivery is taken of a brand new car and there is a latent defect in one or more of the tyres. Such circumstances might well be accepted as special reasons, but the general rule is that ignorance of the defect will not, in itself, amount to a special reason because there is an obligation on the driver, as there is on all motorists, to ensure that his motor vehicle is roadworthy.

It is hoped that the cases set out above and the general comments will be of some assistance, particularly in appreciating the golden rule that in order to avoid compulsory endorsement, or compulsory disqualification, reasons advanced to the court must be special to the offence and not to the offender.

Mitigating circumstances

We have examined the problems arising when a motorist is faced with compulsory disqualification (and disqualification in general) except concerning that area which, perhaps, most affects us – the "totting-up" disqualification. When we enter this area of law we are not concerned with the narrow arguments put forward as special reasons and which relate only to the offence and not the offender. In the case of mitigating circumstances the court is entitled to take into account any matter which satisfies the justices that they ought to mitigate the normal consquences of conviction and that means, in this context, disqualification.

DISQUALIFICATION AND PREVIOUS ENDORSEMENTS

Mitigating circumstances

The problem facing a motorist liable to compulsory disqualification has been examined. Section 93(3) of the Road Traffic Act also requires that there should be compulsory disqualification when a motorist is convicted of an offence for which his licence is ordered to be endorsed and the occasion when he committed the offence falls within three years of two earlier convictions, for which his licence was also ordered to be endorsed. One is always, in these cases, talking about the date of the commission of the offence in respect of the third endorsement and the date of the conviction in respect of the two earlier endorsements. The section goes on to say that the court must disqualify for at least six months, unless it is satisfied that there are circumstances which can be accepted as mitigating the normal consequences of conviction.

It is, therefore, necessary to keep in mind that:

(1) the court is required by law to disqualify for at least six months and that this is compulsory; unless

(2) the court itself is satisfied that there are mitigating circumstances; and

(3) even if there are mitigating circumstances, how far down the line of mitigation do they operate?

Let us consider (3) first. A court might well accept that there are mitigating circumstances and yet still disqualify for a period of less than six months. Clearly, therefore, one must appreciate that the greater the mitigation the shorter the disqualification (even down to no disqualification at all).

The House of Lords discussed this matter in the case of *Lambie* v. *Woodage* [1972] 2 All E.R. 462. In that case they said that section 93 was aimed at the motorist who commits comparatively trivial offences regularly. In saying this they are observing that whenever a motorist has his licence endorsed he is automatically liable to discretionary disqualification, even though he has never previously had his licence endorsed. The "totting-up" provisions, in effect, give a motorist an opportunity to reform himself, as concerns his driving. In the case quoted the motorist concerned had been convicted by magistrates on a third offence of speeding. He argued before the magistrates that his two previous speeding endorsements were placed upon his licence for speeds of only 34 and 37 m.p.h. respectively. The magistrates accepted this as mitigation and did not disqualify him. As a result an appeal was lodged and it eventually reached the House of Lords.

The question before the House of Lords was really concerned with whether or not the evidence placed before the magistrates as to the previous speeds was admissible. They ruled that it was. They were very careful not to answer another obvious question: whether or not the proposition put before the magistrates could be called mitigating circumstances. One cannot help but wonder what their answer would have been had the question been asked; but it is suggested that it is now generally accepted that the triviality of previous offences is not, in itself, a mitigating circumstance. It is very much a question for the court to answer.

Mitigating circumstances must, of necessity, be wider than special reasons in that more often than not they will relate to the offender rather than the offence. The fact that a man might lose his job if disqualified is not a special reason but can certainly amount to a mitigating circumstance.

Let us look at what have been accepted as mitigating circumstances.

Hardship

Hardship is one of the more common grounds put before

courts as to why a defendant should not suffer disqualification. In the case of *Baker* v. *Cole* [1971] 3 All E.R. 680 it was said that magistrates were perfectly entitled not to disqualify under the "totting-up" provisions where the defendant:

(1) was a craftsman;

(2) was employed on a type of work which was not readily available within the town where he lived;

(3) could not be driven to his place of employment;

(4) lived too far away from his place of employment to walk;

(5) could not cycle to work because of an injury;

(6) could not use public transport because it was not running at times when he required to be at his work.

To disqualify him would cause him to be dismissed from his work and this was held up to be excessive hardship.

One of the most troublesome problems facing courts is where the driver depends very much upon his licence. This can be because he or she is disabled or where the defendant drives for a living. He might, for example, be a commercial traveller, or a lorry driver, and to be disqualified would again be tantamount to being dismissed from his job. The questions the court will want to examine are as follows.

(1) Will he really lose his job if disqualified for, perhaps, a six-month period?

(2) If he will lose his job if disqualified for six months, will he necessarily lose his job if disqualified for a shorter period?

(3) If he is a commercial traveller and only selling locally can he perhaps use public transport, a bicycle, or be conveyed by another member of the firm?

In the case of a person who is disabled the court will, no doubt, examine the extent of his disability. Furthermore, the area in which he lives might be very important. If he lives in a town he could probably use public transport, whereas if he lives in a country district public transport might not be readily available.

All these examples are examples of hardship that would be caused to the defendant if he were disqualifed. Even hardship is relative and must not be confused with inconvenience. Again the greater the hardship the more likely it is that a defendant will not suffer disqualification at all. The golden rule seems to be to keep in mind that the section requires the court to start at six months and perhaps move upwards. Mitigating circumstances, if accepted, would require the court to move down what is, in effect, a sliding scale.

It is also pertinent to note that if Parliament had intended that certain drivers should be given particular preferential treatment then it would have said so. For example, Parliament could very easily have written into the statute special provisions concerning disabled drivers. It did not and, therefore, one must presume that they at least start equal to other drivers in that they must suffer the normal consequences to their actions. On the other hand, their disability can properly be put forward to court as a mitigating circumstance, provided that it does indeed mitigate. In the same way one can properly argue that a lorry driver would suffer greater hardship if disqualified than a "week-end casual driver", but the argument is often also advanced that the more professional a driver the greater the care he should take of his licence. At the very least he should be expected to exercise the same standard as any other reasonable driver and, therefore, suffer the same consequences for his actions.

It might be worth mentioning that a court will often exercise discretion in the defendant's favour on the grounds of hardship where, for example, the serious accident in which he was involved, as a consequence of his own carelessness, has resulted in serious injuries to himself and he will not be able to drive a motor vehicle for some considerable time.

Triviality of offence

The decisions of the courts seem to imply that triviality, in itself, is not a mitigating circumstance in that endorsement/disqualification follows the event regardless of degree.

Careless driving is careless driving. Speeding is speeding. Nevertheless, one can properly argue that, in the same way that an aggravating circumstance (e.g. a high speed) can increase a penalty, triviality can go some way to reducing a penalty.

One is not, however, always able to extend this argument to a minimum penalty (which is imposed as a result of the offence being committed rather than with reference to why the offence was committed). It is, nevertheless, submitted that triviality, coupled with other circumstances, can amount to a mitigating circumstance, e.g. where a defendant after an accident gives sufficient particulars for the police to trace him whilst at the same time not fully complying with the strict technicalities of exchanging names and addresses, etc.

Carelessness on the part of the defendant, or the reliance he placed upon another person, can sometimes be put before the court as mitigation, e.g. failure to read a policy of insurance properly, or relying upon someone else to renew.

General considerations

Interval between offences

A long gap between the two previous endorsements and the latest offence can be put before the court as a mitigating circumstance. This seems to be in line with the decision of *Baker* v. *Cole*, in that section 93 is aimed at the persistent, petty motoring offender.

Several offences in one incident

It is not uncommon for a defendant to find himself facing a number of summonses which arise out of what is effectively one incident, e.g. a separate summons for each defective tyre on a motor vehicle. The court might properly decide that four defective tyres are four times more dangerous than one defective tyre but this is at least arguable. On the other hand, the court might well decide that six months' disqualification consecutively for each of the four endorsements ordered would be too harsh a penalty. They might consider a disqualification of less than two years in total justified.

A case on this point is *R.* v. *Sixsmith, ex parte Morris* [1966] 3 All E.R. 473 in which it was held that a person convicted before a court (at a third hearing) of a number of offences – in particular if they arise out of the same incident – can properly argue that the separate summonses can, if necessary, be regarded as one in the sense that the court can either (1) not disqualify on some, or (2) order a shorter disqualification on each. It should be noted, however, that if the court orders a shorter disqualification on each "totting" offence then they must still run consecutively. "Totting-up" disqualifications *cannot* run concurrently. For endorsement purposes only, four endorsements placed upon a licence on one occasion (that is at one court hearing) count as only one endorsement.

Previous good driving record

It is sometimes argued that one must weigh the two previous endorsements shown on the defendant's licence against his previous good driving record. For example, the defendant might drive many thousands of miles each year and may have done so for several years. His two previous endorsements may have arrived within a short space of time after many years of motoring. The previous endorsements might have been for comparatively trivial offences. There might also be the argument of a long unblemished driving record and a substantial gap between his present offence and the two previous endorsements.

All of these are, at first sight, good points; but the court must also bear in mind that Parliament has provided a system of "totting-up" endorsements relative to the period of time in which offences must not be repeated. It has not provided a system relative to mileage. Furthermore, the more miles a person drives and the more necessary the licence to drive is to the driver can be all the more reason for him to avoid a third endorsement.

To a large extent the driver before the court for a third endorsement is (usually but not always) a volunteer. He opted to come before the court as a result of his own actions and with knowledge of the consequences. This only underlines the need to examine most carefully whether there are any circumstances at all which might mitigate. If there are then they *must* be put before the court because the court at the final analysis has a discretion towards the "totting-up" cases.

SUSPENSION OF DISQUALIFICATION PENDING APPEAL

The court which imposes a disqualification has unfettered discretion to suspend its operation pending the result of any appeal. This would include an appeal to the Divisional Court of the High Court of Justice and an appeal to the Crown Court (*see* Appendix I). In exercising their discretion the court will usually consider such points as:

(1) whether the plea was one of "Guilty" or "Not guilty";

(2) in the case of a short disqualification, whether or not it might amount to a denial of justice to refuse an application when there is a possibility of an appeal being successful.

Nevertheless, it is a discretion lying with the court and it can clearly, therefore, operate against an applicant as well as in the applicant's favour.

Written notice of appeal must be received by the court, within the statutory time limit, before suspension of the disqualification pending appeal is ordered.

If the disqualification is suspended pending appeal and subsequently the appeal is not successful then the disqualification will re-commence from the date the result of the appeal is announced.

REMOVAL OF DISQUALIFICATION

A final question remaining to be answered is, "I have been disqualified – can I get my licence back before the normal expiry date of the disqualification?" Section 95 of the Road Traffic Act 1972 provides the answer.

(1) If the disqualification is for less than four years then an application can be made after two years of the disqualification has expired.

(2) If the disqualification is for four years but less than ten years then application can be made to remove the dis-

qualification after half the period has expired.

(3) If the disqualification is anything from ten years to life then an application can be made to remove the disqualification after five years have expired.

Clearly this section prevents an application to remove any disqualification which is for two years or less. Consecutive disqualifications are separate periods. If, for example, a motorist is disqualified for twelve months, twelve months and twelve months consecutively then at first sight one could argue that this is three years' disqualification because that is the practical effect. The fact of the matter is, however, that the second disqualification does not begin to run until the first disqualification has ended and similarly the third disqualification does not begin to run until the second disqualification has ended. Therefore, there are three separate twelve-month disqualifications, each of them, in effect, self-contained. A motorist in this unfortunate situation cannot apply for removal of any of the three disqualifications before their normal expiry date, whereas if he had been disqualified for a total of three years for one offence, or perhaps for three years on all three but concurrent disqualifications, then he could have applied after the expiration of two years.

It is possible to make more than one application to remove a disqualification. If a motorist applies to a court for a disqualification to be removed and is unsuccessful then a further application can be made. It might well be wise for the motorist to have some additional grounds to place before the court on the second or third application, although presumably the expiration of a further period of disqualification might, in itself, persuade the court that the time is now right, whereas on the earlier application it was not.

Crown Court disqualifications must be removed by the location of the Crown Court which imposed the disqualification. Disqualifications imposed by a magistrates' court must be removed by the court which imposed the disqualification, although not necessarily by the same justices.

Prior to 1974 a person convicted of driving whilst disqualified had to suffer compulsory disqualification and any disqualification imposed for driving whilst disqualified was to run consecutively to any other disqualification then in force. The law was, however, amended and the present position is that any defendant suffering disqualifications imposed under the previous Act can now apply for the removal of such disqualifications and the court has a discretion to order removal.

CHAPTER 7

Legal advice and legal aid

LEGAL ADVICE AND LEGAL AID

Legal advice and legal aid are available by law to people of limited means who could not otherwise afford the services of a solicitor or barrister. Motoring offenders are just as entitled to apply for legal aid and to receive legal advice as are those who offend against other parts of the criminal law. The Act which governs this topic is the Legal Aid Act 1974 and the several regulations made thereunder. It is only proposed to deal with the matter in general terms in order to guide any motorist who might wish to obtain legal advice as to the necessary preliminary steps. Once the motorist has reached the stage of interview with a solicitor then there will be an opportunity to deal with any finer points.

LEGAL ADVICE

Any person wishing to obtain legal advice is entitled to attend at the office of a solicitor operating under the provisions of the Legal Aid Scheme. Lists of such solicitors are available at Court Houses and Citizens' Advice Bureaux and information can be obtained from any of the local Law Societies. The public library is another source of information. Solicitors operating the Scheme also use a visual aid in the form of a small notice placed on the front of their office building where it can be seen by passing members of the public. Look for this sign, which is illustrated overleaf.

In money terms, a solicitor bound by the Scheme can offer advice for up to £25. The amount the client pays depends upon his or her financial resources. If, for example, a person

is in receipt of supplementary benefits then they could expect to receive the advice free. It is possible for a person in employment to obtain free legal advice, depending upon a mathematical formula, which in turn depends upon income and outgoings.

Advice does not normally extend to legal representation in court. It might well be that a motorist is involved in an incident concerning his motor vehicle where court proceedings are not even contemplated. There might have been a collision with another vehicle, with neither motorist at fault, and yet advice is often essential because of civil claims, etc. It might also be the other motorist who has offended against the road traffic law; advice might still be necessary for the innocent motorist for a variety of reasons. Advice, therefore, is quite distinct from the other area of the Legal Aid Act, "representation", which is dealt with in another paragraph.

The procedure for obtaining legal advice could not be more simple. Once at the solicitor's office it is the solicitor who will take the necessary details in order to decide whether you qualify to receive free legal advice under the Scheme, or whether you are covered by the Scheme at all.

LEGAL AID

An application can be made for legal aid whenever a prosecution has been commenced. This does not mean that one must wait until the court hearing. The reverse is true. As soon as a motorist is charged with a road traffic offence, or has received a summons, then an application for legal aid can be made. There is, of course, no point in applying for legal aid at notice of intended prosecution stage because it is uncertain whether a prosecution will, in fact, result. Legal advice might, in appropriate cases, still be necessary, but legal aid usually is not. That is the practical situation. But how does one set about obtaining a legal aid order?

The motorist can obtain the necessary application forms from any magistrates' court (that is, from the office of the clerk to the justices). Where the police have charged a motorist following arrest, then the necessary forms can usually be obtained from the police station. If not, then it is common practice for the police to serve an explanatory memorandum as to the procedure to be followed in order to obtain legal aid.

Usually there will be at least two forms to complete. One is a formal application setting out certain personal details and at the same time allowing the motorist to put into writing any special circumstances which warrant his being granted legal aid. If the columns relating to special circumstances are left blank then it should come as no surprise to find that a refusal will generally follow. A committee sat some years ago under the chairmanship of the Lord Chief Justice. That committee put forward certain guidelines as to what would normally be considered to be special circumstances. These are set out below.

(1) The charge is a grave one in the sense that the accused is in real jeopardy of losing his liberty or livelihood or suffering serious damage to his reputation.

(2) The charge raises a substantial question of law.

(3) The accused is unable to follow the proceedings and state his own case because of his inadequate knowledge of English, mental illness or other mental or physical disability.

(4) The nature of the defence involves the tracing and interviewing of witnesses or expert cross-examination of a witness for the prosecution.

(5) Legal representation is desirable in the interest of someone other than the accused, as, for example, in the case of sexual offences against young children, when it is undesir-

able that the accused should cross-examine the witness in person.

Having considered the special circumstances, the Legal Aid Act requires that the application should be scrutinised as to whether or not legal aid is necessary from the financial point of view. For this purpose there *must* be a completed statement of means. This must be completed in writing and there is a penalty provided where an applicant recklessly, or knowingly, makes a false statement. The statement of means sets out sufficient details of income and outgoings so as to allow a calculation to be made as to whether or not the applicant's finances merit a grant of legal aid.

In assessing financial resources allowances are automatically made on a set scale depending upon whether the applicant is married or single and his or her special commitments. It is not proposed to deal in detail with the scale of allowances. For the purpose of this summary it will, no doubt, be sufficient to state that the Legal Aid Act provides as follows:

> "Where it appears desirable in the interest of justice to make a legal aid order, such an order shall not be refused if:
>
> *(a)* the applicant, or spouse with whom the applicant is living, is in receipt of a supplementary pension or allowance payable under the Ministry of Social Security Act 1966; or
>
> *(b)* the applicant's resources at the date of the application which are immediately available do not exceed, in the case of a single person £70 and in the case of a married person £110; or
>
> *(c)* where the applicant is an infant, the appropriate contributor falls within *(a)* or *(b)* above."

Perhaps it should also be added that in appropriate cases readily available capital will also be taken into account. Again, however, certain minimum sums of available capital are disregarded, as is any interest in the main dwelling house in which the person lives.

Assuming that a statement of means has been submitted

and the calculations disclose that legal aid is necessary, who can then grant it? The answer to this question is that legal aid can either be granted by (1) the justices' clerk; (2) a single justice; and (3) the court. (In the case of a matter appearing before the Crown Court any clerk of the Crown Court has the right to grant legal aid as well as the court itself.)

It might well be that the statement of means is placed before the justices' clerk who is not disposed to grant legal aid. His powers are then limited to either refusing legal aid, subject to the making of a down payment (if the down payment is made then legal aid automatically follows), or referring the matter to a single justice for a decision. The single justice can then either grant legal aid or refuse the application (the refusal being subject to a down payment or outright).

If there is an outright refusal by a single justice or a refusal subject to the making of a down payment by a single justice or justices' clerk, the applicant still has the right to make a further application to a full court. In this case it would be an oral application but supported by the compulsory written statement of means.

COST

Legal aid in criminal proceedings (and for this purpose one is also referring to motoring offences) can be free if the court thinks fit. The appropriate officer of the court (in magistrates' courts this will be the clerk to the justices) has a duty to assess the maximum contribution that a legal aid applicant can be ordered to pay. In some cases this will in practice be a nil contribution and the court will properly decide that legal aid should be free. In other cases, however, the possible maximum contribution might be a substantial sum and indeed might even exceed at first sight the actual costs incurred. The amount actually ordered in the latter example can vary from the full costs incurred down to a nil contribution, in that there is discretion at the hands of the court.

Contribution to defence costs

Whatever the decision of the court as to the question of guilt, it is quite possible for there to be an order that a legally aided defendant should make and pay a contribution towards the costs of his defence. In practice this does not happen very often but there could be circumstances where the court considers that it was the defendant himself who "brought the proceedings upon his own head". In such circumstances the defendant could be ordered to make a contribution or indeed ordered to pay the full costs of his defence if the court saw fit. In the vast majority of cases there is no such order made.

CHAPTER 8

General information

ORDER OF SPEECHES

The procedure followed by magistrates' courts can, to a certain extent, be regulated by the court itself but there are statutory rules of procedure which have to be followed. Whether or not a person summoned for a criminal offence (triable before a magistrates' court) chooses to represent himself or to be represented by a solicitor, the speeches are given in the following order.

(1) On the summary trial of an information, where the accused does not plead guilty, the prosecutor shall call the evidence for the prosecution, and before doing so may address the court.

(2) At the conclusion of the evidence for the prosecution, the accused may address the court, whether or not he afterwards makes an unsworn statement or calls evidence.

(3) At the conclusion of the evidence, if any, for the defence, the prosecutor may call evidence to rebut that evidence.

(4) At the conclusion of the evidence for the defence and any unsworn statement which the accused may make and the evidence, if any, in rebuttal, the accused may address the court if he has not already done so.

(5) Either party may, with the leave of the court, address the court a second time, but where the court grants leave to one party it shall not refuse leave to the other.

(6) Where both parties address the court twice the prosecutor shall address the court for the second time before the accused does so.

NOTICE OF INTENDED PROSECUTION

A question asked over and over again is, "Should I have received a notice of intended prosecution?" The answer, in general terms, is that such a notice is *not* required, except when required to be given under section 179 of the Road Traffic Act 1972, as amended. On the other hand, if it is required and the appropriate notice or warning is not given then it is a bar to a conviction. In other words, a conviction cannot follow if the defendant can satisfy the court that section 179 applies but has not been complied with by the prosecution.

The relevant section (as amended) is as follows.

"Section 179

(1) This section applies to:

(a) any offence under this Act to which it is applied by column 7 of Part 1 of Schedule 4 to this Act;

(aa) any offence under subsection (4) of section 13 of the Road Traffic Regulation Act 1967 (traffic regulation on special roads) consisting of failure to observe a speed limit imposed by regulations under that section; and

(b) any offence under section 77(7) of the Road Traffic Regulation Act, 1967, or punishable by virtue of section 78A of that Act.

(2) Subject to the following provisions of this section and to the provisions of paragraphs 5, 6 and 7 of Part IV of the said Schedule 4, where a person is prosecuted for an offence to which this section applies he shall not be convicted unless either:

(a) he was warned at the time the offence was committed that the question of prosecuting him for some one or other of the offences to which this section applies would be taken into consideration; or

(b) within fourteen days of the commission of the offence a summons (or, in Scotland, a complaint) for the offence was served on him; or

(c) within the said fourteen days a notice of the intended prosecution specifying the nature of the alleged offence and the time and place where it is

alleged to have been committed, was:

(i) in the case of an offence against section 17 or 18 of this Act, served on him;

(ii) in the case of any other offence, served on him or on the person, if any, registered as the keeper of the vehicle at the time of the commission of the offence;

and the notice shall be deemed for the purposes of paragraph *(c)* above to have been served on any person if it was sent by registered post or recorded delivery service addressed to him at his last known address, notwithstanding that the notice was returned as undelivered or was for any other reason not received by him.

(3) The requirement of subsection (2) above shall in every case be deemed to have been complied with unless and until the contrary is proved.

(3A) The requirement of subsection (2) above shall not apply in relation to an offence if, at the time of the ofence or immediately thereafter, an accident occurs owing to the presence on a road of the vehicle in respect of which the offence was committed.

(4) Failure to comply with the requirement of subsection (2) above shall not be a bar to the conviction of the accused in a case where the court is satisfied:

(a) that neither the name and address of the accused nor the name and address of the registered keeper, if any, could with reasonable diligence have been ascertained in time for a summons or, as the case may be, a complaint to be served or for a notice to be served or sent in compliance with the said requirement; or

(b) that the accused by his own conduct contributed to the failure."

Paragraphs 5, 6 and 7 of Part IV of Schedule 4 to the Act read as follows.

"5 Where a person is prosecuted on indictment in England or Wales for an offence to which section 179 does not apply, or (if that section does not apply) as regards which the requirement of section 179(2) has been satisfied, or does not apply, section 179(2) shall not be taken to prejudice any power of the jury on the charge for that offence, if they find him not guilty of it, to find him guilty of an offence against section 2 or 3.

6 In Scotland a person may be convicted of an offence against section 2 by virtue of paragraph (1) or (2) above notwithstanding that the requirement of section 179(2) has not been satisfied as respects that offence.

7 A person may be convicted of an offence against section 3 or 18 notwithstanding that the requirement of section 179(2) has not been satisfied as respects that offence where:

(*a*) the charge for the offence has been preferred against him by virtue of paragraph 4 above, and

(*b*) the said requirement has been satisfied, or does not apply, as respects the alleged offence against section 2 or, as the case may be, section 17."

Notice required

(1) Reckless driving.

(2) Driving without due care and attention.

(3) Driving without reasonable consideration.

(4) Exceeding a statutory speed limit.

(5) Exceeding the speed applicable to a particular type of vehicle.

(6) Proceeding at a speed less than the minimum prescribed.

(7) Reckless or careless riding by cyclists.

(8) Disobedience of *certain* traffic signs and police signals (reference should be made to section 22 of the Road Traffic Act 1972).

(9) Leaving a motor vehicle in a dangerous position (but not to failing to comply with a pedestrian crossing regulation).

(10) Aiding or abetting any of the listed offences.

Notice not required

(1) For offences listed in (1)–(6) above or (8)–(10) above committed by the driver of a tram or trolley operated under statutory powers. (Note, however, that (8) applies to horse drawn vehicles).

(2) Other road traffic offences, even if similar to those contained in the statutory list.

(3) Where at the time of the offence or immediately thereafter an accident occurs owing to the presence on a road of the vehicle in respect of which the offence was committed.

Procedure when notice is required

(1) The defendant must be appropriately warned at the time of the possibility of prosecution for the offence; or

(2) he or she must be served with the summons within fourteen days of the offence; or

(3) the appropriate notice of intended prosecution must be sent by the prosecutor within fourteen days of the offence either to the driver or to the registered keeper of the vehicle, or in cases under ss. 17 or 18 (reckless or careless cycling) then to the rider of the cycle.

APPENDIXES

APPENDIX I:
THE GENERAL LEGAL STRUCTURE

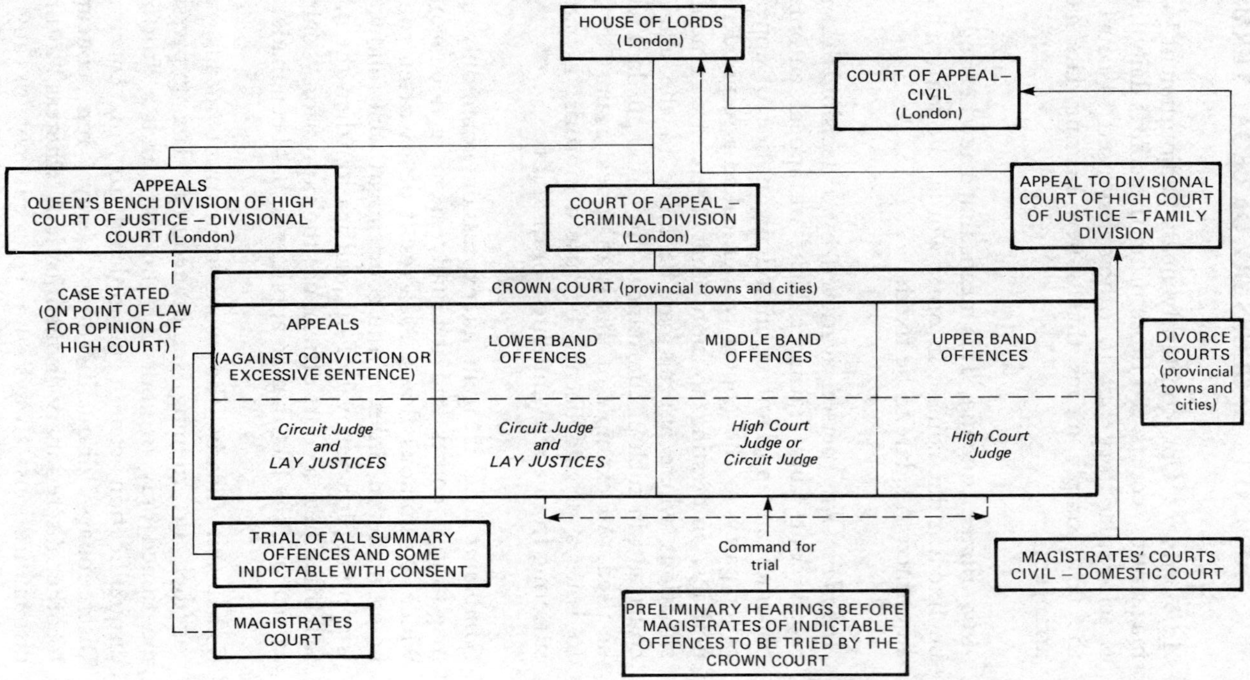

APPENDIX II: GLOSSARY OF LEGAL TERMS

Adjournment One constantly hears "adjournment" used in magistrates' courts. To those using the courts daily the word is self-explanatory but to others less used to court jargon the term simply means that a new hearing date has been arranged.

Adjournment sine die This means that a new hearing date will be fixed in due course. In other words, the matter has been adjourned to a date to be fixed.

Appellant Any person aggrieved by a decision of a magistrates' court and having a right of appeal automatically becomes an appellant upon lodging notice of appeal. The other party to the appeal is then called a respondent. It is, perhaps, interesting to note that there are a number of situations where appeals can be made to the magistrates' court and in such circumstances the term appellant will then be used. An example of this is an appeal against the refusal to issue a driving licence because a motorist is said to be suffering from a relevant illness or disability.

Complaint This is again an expression commonly used in magistrates' courts and it usually means a document from which a summons flows. As a result of a written complaint being made an order of the court might well follow. If one is applying for removal of disqualification then the motorist will often hear a court official use the expression "complaint" as meaning the fact that an application has been made.

Concurrent Clearly the word concurrent means running together or running simultaneously. The expression is mentioned only to underline the point that a "totting-up" disqualification cannot be ordered to run concurrently. Discretionary disqualifications always run concurrently to other discretionary disqualifications, whereas "totting-up" disqualifications always run consecutively to any other type of disqualification(whether compulsory or otherwise).

Consecutive (i.e. one after another) Arising mainly out of the last explanation, it is worth noting that each consecutive disqualification runs separately one from the other. If there are five disqualifications then the second disqualification does not begin to run until the first has been served. This becomes extremely important in the case of "totting-up" disqualifications and the importance can best be illustrated by example.

Let us suppose that a defendant appears before the court for compulsory disqualification under the "totting-up" procedure in respect of five offences. His licence is endorsed in respect of each of the five and he is disqualified for six months on each offence with all disqualifications to run consecutively to each other. This obviously means that he is disqualified for holding or obtaining a driving licence for a total period of two and a half years. Suppose further that he then wishes to apply for removal of disqualification. He cannot! The reason is that you are not permitted to apply for removal of disqualification at an earlier date except where the disqualification exceeds two years. In the circumstances outlined he has been disqualified for five separate periods of six months and, therefore, must serve the total period of disqualification.

Removal of disqualification is dealt with in more detail within the pages of this book.

Court clerk In most courts throughout the country the business of the day is conducted in more than one court room. Each court will be constituted, in the lay justice system, of justices of the peace advised by a court clerk, who will often, of necessity, not be the clerk to the justices. The clerk of the court will, nevertheless, be fully experienced in magisterial law and practice and will often himself (or herself) be a solicitor or barrister. The technical situation is that the clerk to the justices bears ultimate responsibility for advising the magistrates in each court but in practice those functions are carried out under his delegated authority by the clerk of the court concerned.

Defendant/Accused Where an allegation is made against

a person in respect of a road traffic or "criminal" matter, then from the time proceedings are commenced he becomes a "defendant" to those proceedings. On the other hand, if the offence is of such a serious nature that the matter is to be dealt with by the Higher Court, i.e. the Crown Court, then as far as the magistrates are concerned he is an "accused". In the first example he is required to defend an allegation made against him. In the second example he is accused of the allegation and is required to "defend" himself at the court of trial – although he will, in practice, have full opportunity to make explanations to the magistrates when before them for such a serious offence and it might be that the matter never appears before the Crown Court.

The person receiving a summons which has been issued upon a complaint is usually called a "defendant" but occasionally the courts use the expression "respondent". The result is the same.

Informant/Information These expressions are in common use in magistrates' courts. The word "informant" indicates the person who has commenced the proceedings. He might or might not be the actual policeman who is involved with the motorist at the scene, or he could be some other person authorised to commence the proceedings within the prosecutor's office at the police station. His name is important if only because when it appears in the information it gives him a right of audience before the court and he is one of the persons to whom any subsequent notice of appeal must be addressed. The other person is the clerk to the justices at the court concerned.

An "information" is merely a written document (although it can be laid orally) setting out details of the allegations made against the motorist and it is from this document, or from oral information, that a summons is later issued. It is always worth checking to make certain that the information was laid within the appropriate time limit and as a very broad generalisation this is six months from the date of the commission of the offence – although there are exceptions to this rule.

Justice of the Peace In most parts of England and Wales the magistrates' courts operate under what is called a lay justice system. In areas other than that part of England which is the responsibility of the Duchy of Lancaster, justices are appointed to a Commission of the Peace by the Lord Chancellor. The Chancellor of the Duchy of Lancaster directly appoints justices to a Commission of the Peace in that part of England for which he bears responsibility.

One often hears a Justice of the Peace called a "J.P.", or a "magistrate". In fact, the correct title for a lay justice is a "Justice of the Peace".

Justices of the Peace are sometimes themselves solicitors or barristers but they are not appointed to a Commission of the Peace because of their professional qualification. On the other hand, in the larger cities and in the metropolitan area of London there are also stipendiary magistrates (*see below*).

Magistrates' Clerk Each court has a legally qualified person appointed to that court as clerk to the justices. The term "clerk" is, in the author's opinion, grossly misleading in that the holder of the office must, in fact, always be legally qualified for the appointment. Usually the holder of the office is a solicitor or a barrister (and if such then he or she must have been admitted to his profession for not less than five years). The clerk to the justices is often referred to as the "justices' clerk", "magistrates' clerk" and "clerk of the court" as well as by less endearing terms.

The clerk to the justices holds several appointments by virtue of his office, e.g. court collecting officer, clerk to the juvenile court panel, etc. His duties as far as the magistrates themselves are concerned are defined by law, although it is true to say that he has many other executive and administrative duties as well as a number of quasi-judicial duties. An example of his latter role is his power to issue summonses, or to refuse to issue a summons. He is, in effect, the chief legal and administrative officer of the magistrates' court.

His specific advisory duties towards the justices can be found in section 5(3), Justices of the Peace Act 1968 which declares the following.

"It is hereby declared that the functions of a justices' clerk include the giving to the justices to whom he is clerk or any of them, at the request of the justices or justice, of advice about law, practice or procedure on questions arising in connection with the discharge of their functions as justices, including questions arising when the clerk is not personally attending on the justices or justice and that the clerk may, at any time when he thinks he should do so, bring to the attention of the justices or justice any point of law, practice or procedure that is or may be involved in any questions so arising; but the enactment of this sub-section shall not be taken as defining or in any respect limiting the powers and duties belonging to a justices' clerk or the matters on which justices may obtain assistance from their clerk."

Mitigating Circumstances ("Totting-up" Offences) The words "mitigating circumstances" are extremely wide in application. Restricting them to road traffic offences, where the "totting-up" procedure applies, they are still capable of a reasonably wide interpretation. Unlike special reasons, migitigating circumstances can be any circumstance which the court accepts as mitigating the normal consequences of the penalty. Where they can be advanced, a court is perfectly entitled to place them in the scales against the disqualification they would otherwise have imposed and then proceed to consider how much weight they deserve, even to the extent of deciding not to impose any disqualification at all. Again this is dealt with in more detail in other pages of this book.

Remand In the more serious cases when a new hearing date has to be arranged the defendant will hear it announced that the case has been adjourned and that he is remanded to appear on a new date. The word "remand" signifies that he, as the defendant, must appear under threat of a penalty if he does not.

Special reasons Special reasons must be advanced to the court if a motorist wishes to avoid either endorsement of his driving licence or compulsory disqualification. For the purposes of this expression "compulsory disqualification" does not include those under the "totting-up" procedure. On the other hand, it does include the quite common excess alcohol offence as well as other serious offences such as causing death by reckless driving, etc. Whether or not a disqualification is compulsory can be discovered by referring to the Schedule of offences and penalties contained in this book.

In order for a court to find special reasons not to endorse or not to disqualify in the case of compulsory disqualification, then they must, in the broadest general terms, find that there are reasons special to the *offence* and not reasons only special to the offender. It is wise to refer to the chapters dealing with endorsement and disqualification where special reasons are fully explained.

Stipendary magistrate The vast majority of magistrates' courts in England and Wales are part of the lay justice system. In addition there are a substantial number of professional magistrates, particularly in Inner London but also in the larger cities. In the provinces they are appointed by virtue of section 2 of the Administration of Justice Act 1973 which states that it shall be lawful for Her Majesty to appoint a barrister or solicitor of not less than seven years standing to be, during Her Majesty's pleasure, a whole time stipendiary magistrate in any Commission area or areas outside the Inner London area and the City of London. The Lord Chancellor makes the necessary recommendations to Her Majesty.

It is not proposed to deal with the Inner London or the City of London areas in this book and one hopes it will be sufficient to comment that stipendiary magistrates in those areas are also solicitors or barristers.

A stipendiary magistrate is, therefore, a professionally qualified magistrate of not inconsiderable experience. A Justice of the Peace is appointed in a lay capacity and not because of any legal qualifications. The lay justice does, of course, have a professionally qualified clerk to advise on matters of law, practice and procedure whenever necessary.

T.I.C. One normally hears solicitors and court officials using expressions such as "he is asking for fifteen T.I.C.s". The intials T.I.C. stand for "taken into consideration". A court is entitled, in assessing penalty, to take into consideration other offences committed by the defendant, which he admits but in respect of which he has not been formally charged. The penalty imposed by the court upon the defendant will, therefore, reflect the court's attitude to his known and admitted criminal activities.

One does not usually find this occurring in connection with motoring offences, except where the motorist is charged with a "crime"; but, of course, it might be that there is a charge of taking a motor vehicle without the consent of the owner before the court with a request by the defendant for a number of other similar offences to be taken into consideration. The reason why courts are reluctant to allow the practice of taking offences into consideration to creep too far into motoring law is because of the requirement for compulsory endorsement in respect of certain offences and the "totting-up" procedure.

To take an offence into consideration which is endorsable would result in the court not being able to endorse in respect of that particular offence (there being no conviction) and this might subsequently allow the motorist to avoid the natural consequences of committing further motoring offences, e.g. "totting-up" disqualification.

The usual procedure is for the prosecution to list the further offences committed by the defendant upon a standard form. Most forms contain a paragraph stating that the defendant admits the further offences listed. The defendant is required to sign the form. This action is sufficient for the court to act upon the defendant's own request that the further offences be taken into consideration with the offence or offences with which he is charged before the court. Nevertheless it is a matter entirely in the discretion of the court as to whether or not the further offences are taken into consideration. If the court agrees then each offence will be put to the defendant in court and he will again be asked whether he admits or denies them and whether he wishes them to be taken into consideration. If any of the offences are denied then they will not be acted upon by the court.

"Totting-up" This expression is frequently used in magistrates' courts and almost without exception it refers to the fact that the defendant before the court has just been convicted of either his third or fourth (or more) motoring offence which has resulted in his licence being endorsed on at least two previous occasions during the previous three years prior to the date of his present *conviction*. In other words, he is liable to be disqualified for a compulsory period of six months for every endorsable offence for which he now appears before the court and in respect of which he has just been convicted. Each disqualification imposed that day will have to run consecutively to each other and consecutively to any other to which he is already subject. It should be noted that the relevant section states that there will be a minimum period of six months disqualification unless the court finds there are circumstances which mitigate the normal consequences of conviction.

Index

Also published in conjunction
with the RAC

RAC LEARNER DRIVER'S GUIDE

Do you want to pass your driving test and become a safe driver?

This book has been written specifically for learner drivers. It explains, simply and concisely, exactly what the requirements of safe and skilful driving are. Much emphasis is placed on a detailed consideration of the techniques demanded by the driving test, and the reasons for their importance, so that success in the test is readily accessible to all. Appendixes on the Highway Code and Disabled Drivers are included, as are sections dealing with difficult driving conditions.

The author has conducted over 7,000 driving tests.

Harry Jones was for several years a Ministry of Transport Driving Examiner; he then became a Ministry Approved Instructor. He has, therefore, been able to study learners both as they learn to drive and under test conditions and to note their reactions. This opportunity, together with the knowledge of all the techniques which are acceptable to examiners, has resulted in this new approach to driving tuition.

